Arkansas Women
and the Right to ✔ote

Arkansas Women and the Right to Vote

The Little Rock Campaigns, 1868–1920

Bernadette Cahill

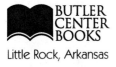

BUTLER
CENTER
BOOKS

Little Rock, Arkansas

The Butler Center for Arkansas Studies
Central Arkansas Library System
100 Rock Street
Little Rock, Arkansas 72201
www.butlercenter.org

First edition: September 2015

ISBN 978-1-935106-82-1
ISBN 978-1-935106-84-5 (e-book)

Manager: Rod Lorenzen
Book and cover designer: H. K. Stewart
Copyeditor: Ali Welky

*Front cover: Suffragists pose in the doorway of the Old State House in Little Rock displaying
the "Great Demand" banner that led the 1913 inaugural suffrage campaign march in
Washington DC. Mabel Vernon (fifth from left) and Alice Paul (second from right), national
organizers for the Congressional Union, are shown with members of the Arkansas branch of
the organization. (From left to right): Mrs. Bernard Hoskins, Mrs. Faith Jarrett, Miss Gertrude
Watkins, Miss Josephine Miller, Mrs. M. Blaisdell, Miss H. Chambers, and Mrs. S. P. Scott.
(Photo courtesy of Sewell-Belmont House Museum, Washington DC)*

Library of Congress Cataloging-in-Publication Data

Cahill, Bernadette.
  Arkansas women and the right to vote : the Little Rock campaigns, 1868-1920 / Bernadette
Cahill. -- First edition.
      pages cm
  Includes bibliographical references.
  ISBN 978-1-935106-82-1 (paperback : alkaline paper) -- ISBN 978-1-935106-84-5 (e-book)
1. Women--Suffrage--Arkansas--Little Rock--History. 2. Suffragists--Homes and haunts--
Arkansas--Little Rock. 3. Suffragists--Arkansas--Little Rock--Biography. 4. Historic
buildings--Arkansas--Little Rock. 5. Historic sites--Arkansas--Little Rock. 6. Little Rock
(Ark.)--History. 7. Little Rock (Ark.)--Biography. 8. Little Rock (Ark.)--Politics and
government. 9. Little Rock (Ark.)--Buildings, structures, etc. I. Title.
  JK1911.A8C24 2015
  324.6'2309767--dc23

                    2015017773

Printed in the United States of America
This book is printed on archival-quality paper that meets requirements of the
American National Standard for Information Sciences, Permanence of Paper, Printed
Library Materials, ANSI Z39.48-1984.

Butler Center Books, the publishing division of the Butler Center
for Arkansas Studies, was made possible by the generosity of Dora
Johnson Ragsdale and John G. Ragsdale Jr.

This book is dedicated to
all the women
who
non-violently
faced down
ridicule,
discrimination
exclusion,
violence,
and
torture
in pursuit of votes for women
from the founding of the United States
to 1920.

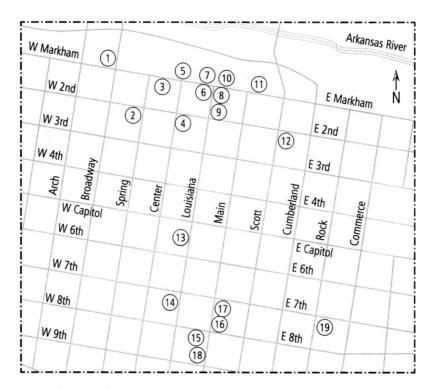

Map Legend

1. City Hall, *500 West Markham Street*
2. Liberty Hall, *Spring and Second Streets (southwest corner)*
3. McDiarmid Block, *313-315, West Markham Street*
4. Equal Suffrage State Central Committee Offices, *221 West Second Street* (Southern Trust Building)
5. The Old State House, *300 West Markham Street*
6. Capital Theater, *200 Block, West Markham Street (south side)*
7. Marion Hotel, *200 Block, West Markham Street (north side)*
8. Capital Hotel, *113–123 West Markham Street*
9. *Woman's Chronicle, 122 West Second Street*
10. Old City Hall, *120–122 West Markham Street*
11. Woman's Christian Temperance Union, *106 East Markham Street*
12. Board of Trade, *Second and Scott Streets*
13. Kempner Theatre, *500 Block, South Louisiana Street*
14. Carnegie Library, *Seventh and South Louisiana Streets*
15. Royal Arcanum Hall, *105 West Eighth Street*
16. *Arkansas Ladies' Journal, 723 South Main Street*
17. YMCA, *717–719, South Main Street*
18. Turner Studio, *814 Main Street*
19. Adolphine Fletcher Terry's Home, *411 East Seventh Street*

Table of Contents

Introduction:
A Lost Opportunity

In 1868, a proposal to include women's voting rights in Arkansas's new constitution was laughed out of debate. That first attempt at women's suffrage in the state occurred at the same time as the adoption of the 14th Amendment to the U.S. Constitution, guaranteeing citizenship and equality specifically to men of all races. It also occurred only a couple of years before the introduction of the 15th Amendment, guaranteeing all men of the nation, regardless of race, the right to vote. If in 1868 a clause giving women the vote *had* been included in its new constitution, Arkansas could have been called the trailblazer state, as it would have been the first state in the Union to guarantee women's equal participation in the political process.

This lost chance of setting an example for the rest of the country to follow and the opportunities thrown away by that failure are sad to contemplate. From Arkansas's inauspicious start toward women's suffrage in 1868 to the successful reaching of the goal by 1920—Arkansas ratified the 19th Amendment in July 1919—the struggle to win equal voting rights for women took more than fifty years. During this time, countless women lived and died excluded from the political process—and many who campaigned for inclusion died before their cause was finally won.[1]

The campaign for votes for women in Arkansas, however, actually took much longer than half a century, for the agitation for women's right to vote in the state cannot be divorced from the national campaigns, which began at the Seneca Falls Convention in New York in 1848. Among the proposals produced at that convention, the most controversial was the right of women to vote. Introduced and passed at the prodding of Elizabeth Cady Stanton, the demand for suffrage was that lady's first and possibly greatest triumph, because it put the issue squarely on the national agenda. Stanton's success was greeted with great hilarity in the press, and the whole campaign, from this first fight to include women's suffrage in the demands of the Seneca Falls Convention right down to the successful national victory in 1920, took seventy-two years. This was the longest civil rights campaign in U.S. history.[2]

That the rights of women are considered civil rights at all tends to give people pause, for the concept of civil rights in the United States in the twenty-first century is virtually synonymous with the rights of African Americans. Yet the history of civil rights in general is much longer and broader than the movement for rights for African Americans that began in the 1950s. With regard to the vote specifically, some women questioned their exclusion at the country's founding and early in the Republic.[3] The question of their participation arose in the succeeding years, particularly with Frances Wright's equality campaign from 1828.[4] With the Seneca Falls Convention in 1848, women launched what became a campaign to win suffrage along with many other reforms for women, such as equal education, equality under the law, and equal employment opportunity. The common denominator of all of these reforms was a protest against the inequality inherent in the segregation into public and private spheres along sex lines. Women's concerns, including the vote, therefore, arose long before the Civil War. By the time of that conflict, "universal suffrage" had become the call of reformers for when slavery was ended.

Before the war, universal suffrage meant all adults, regardless of race or sex. After the war, however, Republicans hijacked the term, applying it to an expanded but extremely limited idea—votes for men only. This warped definition of "universal" became the legislators' new mantra after abolition and excluded half the population from the vote. By 1870, with the forced ratification of the 14th and 15th Amendments to the U.S. Constitution, male suffrage had become a constitutional guarantee and male-only suffrage the fundamental law of the land. At that point, the excluded fifty percent of the population faced continuing their already long-established campaign but in much worse circumstances than before. Women's exclusion from the vote had previously been a matter of custom and prejudice; now it was fundamental law that had to be changed. Women, therefore, had to choose to focus on suffrage as a first step toward complete women's equality.

The notion of women's struggle for civil rights, therefore, is a matter of fact, even if it is largely ignored and usually lost in women's rights slogans. Meanwhile, women's rights have historically been relegated to a lower status than rights for others. Evidence of this is that the history of black civil rights comes to the fore both nationally and locally. For example, my research in Washington DC found that the places where African Americans fought for their civil rights in the nation's capital are clearly marked and honored, complete with labels and a downloadable guide. In Arkansas, Little Rock has its Central High School National Historic Site commemorating the desegregation battles of the 1950s and 1960s, while downtown markers also denote key places where blacks fought to win equality. These historical commemorations are instructive, poignant, and rewarding to see.

By contrast, the idea that women should have equality under the law is still seemingly up for debate, and commemorations of the rights they have won are difficult to come by. Women's history is not only largely ignored, but any woman hunting for the places where women struggled to win the fundamental right of the vote will have a hard time finding them, for those places are largely forgotten. In Washington DC, it is all but impossible to locate where suffragists fought to secure the right of half of the U.S. population to vote. The same holds true in Little Rock. This situation became the impetus for the research in this book, which locates the places in the Arkansas capital city where women struggled for the right to vote, tells the story of the struggle for women in this city to gain the vote, and identifies some of the women who contributed to this most momentous national victory for democracy.

Besides providing information not previously available, this book also will widen awareness. It is important to awaken the idea that the struggle for what is now considered the most basic right of citizenship—to participate in politics through the vote—affects *all* the people of this country, of *all* races and *all* classes. The struggle has been truly diverse and inclusive. Its history, however, is hardly ever presented in that way.

This book also seeks to correct some false historical impressions, such as the situation that leapt out at me when a Little Rock woman seriously interested in history in Little Rock commented to me how terrible it was that "women got the vote even before African Americans." This statement highlights the different notions people hold about civil rights for different groups in the United States. Her use of the word "even" indicates the fact that throughout the national consciousness, the guarantee of civil rights for specific races is uppermost in some people's minds, only secondly considered more important than those for women of all races. Such a comment indicates the perceived hierarchy of the sexes in America.

Yet her statement is also wrong. The simple fact is that black men had a constitutional guarantee of the right to vote from the ratification of the Reconstruction Amendments—the 14th and, in particular, the 15th. After 1870, black men won some elected offices very quickly. By contrast, the first woman to serve in the U.S. Congress, elected in Montana in 1916, was sworn in in 1917—nearly fifty years after the first black man served in Congress. Women finally won ratification of the 19th Amendment guaranteeing them the right to vote only in 1920, fully fifty years *after* black men were given the right by the Reconstruction Amendments.

To say this is not to deny that African Americans—and other races of both sexes—had to fight for many rights after women won the right to vote across the land. It is to highlight the fact that the constitutional guarantees of those rights based on race were not enforced, even though the power to pass laws to enforce them was included in the Reconstruction Amendments. This was a massive dereliction of duty at the federal level that opened the way for the states to devise means to exclude black men (and later black women) from exercising their constitutional right to vote. These exclusionary measures, like the poll tax, cast a wide net and caught many poor whites also. Further, the U.S. Supreme Court made a mockery of the Reconstruction Amendments that guaranteed equal treatment under the law regardless of race, allowing states to adopt other measures to develop and enforce segregation after the Court's *Plessy v. Ferguson* decision.[5] Yet, this is a different situation from what women faced, as winning a right is very different from enforcing one.

All of this racist voter exclusion devised by various states happened concurrently with a state of affairs in which it was fully constitutional nationally to discriminate against women, exclude them from the vote, relegate them to inferior opportunities, and deny them equality.

The two circumstances—women's total exclusion from the polity and Jim Crow laws that hampered the voting of African Americans, among other things—were not unconnected. Susan B. Anthony, the leading suffragist of the nineteenth century, clearly predicted this. In the period of women's civil disobedience and before her own trial after being charged with the criminal act of voting, she had anticipated the repercussions of excluding women by law and judicial decision from the vote, saying: "If we once establish the false principle that United States citizenship does not carry with it the right to vote in every state in this Union, there is no end to the petty freaks and the cunning devices that will be resorted to, to exclude one and another class of citizens from the right of suffrage."[6] The "petty freaks and the cunning devices" were applied to all women long before individual states began to do the same to black men after the Supreme Court declared that voting was not a right of citizenship.[7]

Another point to consider related to the history of civil rights is the consequence of women winning the vote. Women's political clout through utilizing the right to vote starting in 1920—as opposed to political influence beforehand—actually affected and contributed to the progress and success of those later racial struggles and the eradication of legalized discrimination. In other words, how did women winning the vote reinforce from 1920 the clout of African Americans claiming their civil rights? These are important questions, for one almost immediate impact of women winning the vote was that any exclusion from voting rights based on race now doubled the discrimination and the injustice when it extended to, for instance, black women. Another consequence, however, was a doubling of the potential number of foot soldiers to win redress. These facts raise another question: If women had not won the vote in 1920, would the African American civil rights movement of the 1960s have achieved what it did? When the issue of civil rights is seen at its broadest, it becomes clear that women's struggles were influential in gaining civil rights for all.

Women's struggles for the vote had further effects on the race component of civil rights, as individuals linked suffrage and African American civil rights. Adolphine Fletcher Terry of Little Rock is a perfect example. Terry's work in helping to resolve race problems is well known. What is also known is that Terry's first exposure to racial attitudes different from her Southern outlook, which she expressed in conversation at Vassar before the end of the nineteenth century, came from a woman named Lucy Burns of Brooklyn, New York. Terry credited Burns with opening her eyes to new ways of thinking about race.

This anecdote vibrates with import for historians of racial struggles in the United States, but without further knowledge, it would be difficult to understand its full significance—which is that Burns provides the direct link between Arkansas and what were to become the radical suffragists of the twentieth century's second decade. In that decade, this Lucy Burns was one of the most famous women in the country—the same person who, from 1913 on, worked with Alice Paul, the architect of the final campaign that finally won the vote for women in the United States after 144 years of exclusion from the polity. Burns was one of a small group who led women to suffrage success in 1920 and who served more time in prison than any other as a campaigner for the National Woman's Party (NWP) in its successful non-violent campaign to win the federal amendment. She was attacked in public, beaten up in prison, and tortured with forcible feeding while on a hunger strike. Without people like Burns and Paul, one wonders when U.S. women would have won the vote, for without a federal amendment, it was a painfully slow process through the states.

Through Terry, Arkansas women were directly linked to Paul and Burns, and when the NWP came calling to Little Rock, Terry made them welcome, supporting them even in the most difficult times of 1917. It was after suffrage that she became prominent in the matter of racial civil rights in the 1950s and had experience from the former struggle to aid in the latter.

Terry, in fact, never seemed to lose a belief in the power of women as opposed to that of men, even in race matters, if one quote often referred to regarding the desegregation crisis in Little Rock in 1957–58 is true:

There were other calls from Miss Adolphine in the months that followed, and nothing sanguine to report as the city lurched through the bizarre season of occupation by federal troops. We came, finally, to the foreordained when the governor padlocked the city's high schools and turned away all of Little Rock's children, white and colored alike. It was then that Miss Adolphine sighed and said, 'I see. The men have failed again. I'll have to send for the young ladies.'[8]

As is obvious from this discussion, it is impossible to talk of civil rights for women in the United States without the subject of race coming up. The simple fact is that the two issues are tightly woven together. But these interlinked topics are too often treated unequally. While it is common to raise questions of racial civil rights both today and historically, it is much less common or acceptable to raise questions of gender-based civil rights both today and historically. While African American history rightly has institutions to honor it, women's history is still largely ignored, with no bricks-and-mortar national women's history museum, even as Women's History Month in March and Women's Equality Day on August 26 every year receive minimal attention. Women, in fact, still do not have equality before the law in the United States. The Equal Rights Amendment (ERA), which would guarantee equality in law on account of sex, stalled in 1982 at thirty-five state ratifications, and attempts today to re-start the process seem to face insurmountable obstacles. Meanwhile many Americans have believed for years that the ERA was long ago ratified.[9] Lack of awareness and interest in women's history is one of those obstacles.

Arkansas women did not win equal voting rights through a state amendment. They won it in 1920 with a federal amendment. The overall struggle, involving both national and state campaigns, was huge. The enormity of the struggle alone merits its commemoration in the histories. History, however, is not just about people and events; it is also about places. Something is always added to people's understanding of the past if they get to see where history happened: just consider what it feels like at the Lincoln Memorial in Washington DC, or Daley Plaza in Dallas, or the Little White House in Georgia. But this issue is a two-way street. Finding out what happened in the past in places that are familiar but which were never linked up to history in this way before changes the way people look at those places.

This book, therefore, is ultimately about place and about changing individuals' perceptions of Little Rock to include the history of women. From knowing where certain women worked to win the most important civil right of all for fifty percent of the population, it is a short step to honor the full history of the Arkansas capital city, to recognize its previously unknown richness, and to appreciate the role of those individual struggles in the history of the whole nation.

This book deals with more than twenty specific sites where women fought for the right to vote. Unfortunately, only a few are still extant. In addition, the streetscapes in which the women's activities took place have changed and photographs have not yet emerged for all of the sites. This is history very likely lost. The information contained in this book, although limited, is based on original research and is a valuable addition to the available knowledge of Arkansas's capital city.

As many of the locations are close to each other, I have organized the chapters as a potential walking tour from one site to another around Arkansas's capital, starting with City Hall. Each chapter tells the role of the people and events connected with the site. Each chapter is self-contained and is readable individually. Together, however, they give a history of the suffrage campaign in Arkansas from 1868 to 1920, demonstrating the importance of the local campaigns to the national

success. A bibliography also gives suggestions for further reading. For the first time, a walk through Little Rock with this guide can help restore to life that period when women—in contravention of all custom—took to the streets and campaigned so that they would be allowed to take part in the political process, paving the way once more for battles over many of the same issues, but now in a racial context, in the 1950s and 1960s.

(Below) Little Rock downtown panorama, looking north. (Conneaut, Ohio, Haines Photo Co.), ca. 1910. (Courtesy of Library of Congress Prints and Photographs Division)

Chapter 1:
City Hall—Did She or Didn't She?
500 West Markham Street

Little Rock City Hall opened in 1908 at the corner of Markham and Broadway. Originally, a dome crowned it, but that was removed in the 1950s because voters did not want to pay for repairs. City Hall was prominent early on in the history of women's suffrage in Little Rock when, as the *History of Woman's Suffrage* relates, in 1913 the Women's Political Equality League began to meet there: "In October, 1913, Mrs. O. F. Ellington was elected president of [the Women's Political Equality League in Little Rock]…[and]…the executive board secured the parlors of the City Hall [for its meetings]….Important local, State and national affairs were studied and discussed and prominent State and national speakers addressed that eager body of women."[10] Unfortunately, this history provides no further details of the "prominent State and national speakers."

In 1917, the same building became important as the votes-for-women campaign in Arkansas ratcheted up, specifically when Mabel Vernon spoke there on a trip around the country during a two-month congressional break. At least, local newspapers reported that she was *going* to speak in City Hall. It is unclear in local sources if she actually did, for neither of the city's two newspapers, the *Democrat* and the *Gazette*, reported on such a meeting after the event they publicized.

The answer to this Arkansas mystery comes from the national story of suffrage. While relating the history of the November 1917 tour by members of the NWP across the country to explain their picketing and hunger strikes, the NWP's historian later recorded, "Suddenly, while everything was apparently going smoothly, audiences large, indignantly sympathetic, actively protective, change came. Everywhere obstacles were put in the way of the speakers. That this was the result of concerted action on the part of the authorities was evident from the fact that within a few days four speakers in different parts of the country felt this blocking influence. In Arkansas they recalled Mabel Vernon's permit for the Court House"[11] Mabel Vernon was a big name from the National Woman's Party (NWP), the organization campaigning for a federal constitutional amendment guaranteeing women voting rights in all states.

The NWP since its early days had set a new pace for suffrage action. Its work began in January 1913 as the Congressional Committee of the National American Woman Suffrage Association (NAWSA); a year later it was the separate Congressional Union and finally became the NWP. When its leader, Alice Paul, took on the work, the NAWSA had largely been a genteel organization of older women who ignored federal politics and pursued women's suffrage through state campaigns, organizing marches but largely lobbying for votes for women while being firmly set on womanly decorum. Their work had yielded little. Wyoming entered the Union as a state in 1890 with women's suffrage intact— women had already had the vote there since 1869. But, by 1913, women had either won equal suffrage or secured it at entry to the Union in only nine states.[12]

Alice Paul of New Jersey—like others such as Lucy Burns of New York and Mabel Vernon of Delaware—was from a new generation of women who were not content to wait for men to grant women the vote: they began to demand it and began to lobby the Congress and the president, aiming for a federal amendment that would bypass the long, tedious state-by-state process. Paul and Burns began the crusade with a huge suffrage parade in Washington DC on March 3, 1913—the day before President Wilson's inauguration. The ground-breaking political parade of women and the ensuing riot against the women stole the new president's thunder and put Alice Paul and Lucy Burns and their succeeding organizations on the map.

Mabel Vernon was an early organizer of key NWP protests, including one in December 1916 when she helped unfurl a banner in the House of Representatives when President Wilson talked of legislation that would have allowed adult male Puerto Ricans to vote.[13] Parades and protests set the pace for women's suffrage campaigns, putting out of joint the collective noses of the NAWSA membership. By 1916, the NAWSA, playing catch-up under the direction of a new president, Carrie Chapman Catt, had modified its policy slightly, aiming to win whatever voting rights women could get, partial or otherwise. They sought these rights both in their states and, if possible, federally.

The NAWSA refused to work with the NWP, objecting to its tactics, which they called militant. The NWP, in fact, was not militant: it demonstrated with strength, not violence. Following Paul's Quaker philosophy, the members were adamantly non-violent—to the extent of absorbing the violence, both verbal and physical, of any opponents to their methods in order to maintain their philosophy and their campaign. Their iconic symbol became the "silent sentinels" standing outside the gates of the White House displaying banners proclaiming not only their primary demand—votes for women—but the words of the president, displaying his hypocrisy for all to see.

The militants were, in fact, those who attacked the silent sentinels outside the White House. Later, the militants were the authority figures who had the women under their power when illegal arrests began. Up to November 1917, when Mabel Vernon spoke in Little Rock, the most "militant" action the NWP had taken was to continue its campaign for suffrage even when the United States joined World War I in 1917. The most "violent" action was to break two windows—one to get air into the obscene condemned prison where the suffragists were held illegally and another to allow them to leave a locked room in the U.S. Capitol where—again—they were imprisoned illegally.[14]

November 1917 was a busy month for women's suffrage in Little Rock. One of the state's leading suffragists, Mrs. T. T. Cotnam, was welcomed home triumphantly with Miss Josephine Miller and Miss Gertrude Watkins. These Arkansans had contributed to victory in New York, by which women there had finally won the vote. This was an important strategic victory for women across the country because it brought yet another hugely populous state into the women's suffrage fold. It had almost become a political tipping point—but not quite.

The tipping point was provided by Alice Paul, the NWP, and women such as Mabel Vernon and her advance guard Jane Pincus, who braved the icy reception of Little Rock's women to tell the true story of how the women who were fighting for the primary civil right of citizenship were being treated by the authorities in Washington DC.

Little Rock's City Hall was the third venue for meetings of the Little Rock Political Equality League after 1911. (Courtesy of Butler Center for Arkansas Studies, Little Rock, Arkansas)

In 1917, city fathers objected to the "Silent Sentinels" of the NWP in Washington DC and canceled Mabel Vernon's meeting in City Hall. Yet the picketers included a woman from Arkansas. Pauline Floyd of El Dorado, on the extreme right of the photo, was a member of the first-ever group that headed for the White House on January 10, 1917, from National Woman's Party Headquarters to picket President Wilson and win his support for votes for women. Later that year, many such peaceful picketers were imprisoned and went on hunger strikes for political rights. (Records of the National Woman's Party, Courtesy of Library of Congress Manuscript Division)

Local suffragists who were members of the NAWSA warned Mabel Vernon, national suffrage campaigner and former suffrage prisoner, that she was not welcome in Little Rock in November 1917. They disapproved of the NWP's tactics and lobbied behind the scenes for the recall of her permit to speak in City Hall. (Source: *Arkansas Gazette*, November 9, 1917, 1.)

Chapter 2:
Liberty Hall—Dr. Anna Howard Shaw Speaks, Spring and Second Streets (southwest corner)

After the United States declared war on Germany in April 1917, the National American Woman Suffrage Association (NAWSA) diverted much of its energy to war work. In Little Rock, suffragist Josephine Miller, a Red Cross nurse and national representative of the NAWSA, began organizing women into war-work groups in Desha, Chicot, Ashley, Union, Bradley, and Dallas counties.[15] The structure of these organizations echoed the re-organization of Arkansas's suffrage groups following Arkansas women's win of primary voting rights in March 1917.[16]

Long before the start of World War I—late in 1915—a major change had occurred in the NAWSA when the Reverend Anna Howard Shaw stepped down from the presidency after eleven years. Shaw—whose parents had brought her to the United States from England when she was four—had virtually a pioneer start in the United States in northern Michigan, then struggled as a teacher and seamstress before she became an ordained minister and later a medical doctor. She embraced suffrage ardently for decades. After the NAWSA presidency, she became chair of the Women's Committee of the United States Council of National Defense in April 1917. As such—but also heralded as a leading suffragist—in April 1918, she made a brief visit to Little Rock to talk in Liberty Hall about war work for women.[17]

"The greatest crime that has been perpetrated towards women is that they have not been allowed to develop their powers, to meet life and to bear its responsibilities," Dr. Shaw said. If women had not done what men had done, it was because American society, law, and politics had blocked them. She went on, "The very first measure that Congress should pass is votes for women in order that they be made *bona fide* citizens of the United States. After the government has made us citizens, then it has the right to conscript us to service."[18]

Shaw's reference here was to a failed law case brought by women to establish their right to vote under the Reconstruction Amendments. In 1875, the Supreme Court had held that citizenship in the United States did not confer the right to vote.[19] This limitation at the time applied to every citizen in theory, but in practice only to women. The decision, however, threw the doors open for discriminatory state voting laws, even though discrimination in voting for males, including discrimination that affected one race more than another, had been banned under the Fifteenth Amendment to the U.S. Constitution in 1870.

During the war, two very different groups with an interest in the vote crossed paths at Liberty Hall. Around the time Shaw spoke there, the hall also served as temporary housing for Puerto Ricans brought to town to work at a plant established by the federal government to manufacture picric acid for the war. The project was soon discontinued, but 176 of about 1,500 Puerto Ricans died of various causes. A lone marker in Calvary Cemetery commemorates them.[20]

Many Puerto Ricans were in the United States at that time because President Wilson's signature on March 2, 1917, had made them U.S. citizens when the Jones-Shafroth Act created a U.S. protectorate of their island. They made a 75,000-strong pool of new workers in a nation ramping up its war industries. They also represented an increase in the electorate, for Puerto Rican males twenty-one years and over had had the right to vote since 1904. The debate preceding this measure, therefore, had raised the ire of suffragists facing the prospect of brand-new male Americans getting the right to vote as an outright gift, even as lawmakers continued to refuse to countenance the idea of enfranchising female Americans who had been excluded from full citizenship since the nation's founding.

Some Washington DC suffragists protested. On December 5, 1916, President Wilson addressed Congress, but it was reported that "men's needs and men's business were the subject of the President's concern.

There was not one word devoted to legislation directly concerning women." When the president began "in the midst of the message, so empty for women," to speak of Puerto Rico, members of the National Woman's Party (NWP), strategically positioned on the House balcony, unfurled a banner demanding to know, "Mr. President, what will you do for woman suffrage?" The protest, the first of its kind, brought women's suffrage spectacularly into the public eye.[21]

Anna Howard Shaw and the NAWSA, however, disapproved of such behavior. Shaw's advocacy of war work in Little Rock was a clear example of the much less assertive—but much less effective—method that America's women had adopted for decades in an attempt to win the vote. This had included the loss of momentum and clout when women had suspended their own equal rights campaign at the start of the Civil War—a decision that led directly to lawmakers' refusal to include women in the voting clauses of the Fourteenth and Fifteenth Amendments at the end of the war.

The Jones-Shafroth Act, however, did not allow inhabitants of Puerto Rico to vote for president, as they did not belong to a full-fledged state. They experienced a compromised citizenship through voting inequalities, just as American women had always done in full states. In Little Rock, the paths of these two disadvantaged groups toward suffrage briefly intersected.[22]

Liberty Hall, according to one source, was "a temporary auditorium in Little Rock."[23] It was remembered in a 1970s article in Little Rock as "the large building…on the higher ground known as Donkey Hill, at 2nd and Spring Streets, used as a meeting place during World War I."[24] In 1920, it was described as at "Spring Street, s w corner 2nd."[25] Opposite the rear of the Pulaski County Court House, today the location is a parking lot.

Dr. Anna Howard Shaw, former president of the NAWSA and chair of the Women's Committee of the United States Council of National Defense, visited Little Rock in April 1917 to speak on war work, when she also argued strongly for suffrage. She is pictured here ca. 1910. (Courtesy Library of Congress Prints and Photographs Division)

Chapter 3:
Suffragists Meet—but Where?
West Markham Street (1889)

Clara McDiarmid appears frequently in all the accounts of the nineteenth-century campaigns for civil rights for women in Arkansas. She was a real estate agent not only involved in the Woman's Christian Temperance Union (WCTU), which campaigned for prohibition of alcohol and took on support for women's suffrage too, but was also one of the founders and the first president of the Arkansas Equal Suffrage Association established in Little Rock in 1888.[26] McDiarmid, the historical accounts state, provided an office for the Arkansas suffrage association throughout the 1890s,[27] and while the WCTU thrived, the women's suffrage movement struggled and ultimately faded away after McDiarmid died in 1899.[28]

But the historical accounts refer only vaguely to "an office on West Markham" and "opposite the Old State House." But where exactly? The location seems a mystery. But the mystery is actually easy to solve. The 1890 Little Rock City Directory states quite clearly that the "McDiarmid Block" was at 313–315 West Markham.[29]

Miss Ida Joe Brooks, whose speech on suffrage in Arkansas at the Massachusetts Annual Suffrage Association was reported in 1889, gave additional information: "We have a staunch friend in our president, Mrs. McDiarmid, who expresses her faith in words like these: 'If the various societies of women cannot afford to pay rent for quarters, I will put up a building for their exclusive use.'"[30]

In fact, the office on West Markham was officially opened for the WCTU in late 1889. That September, the *Arkansas Democrat* reported that Mrs. McDiarmid "will donate two rooms [on the second floor] of the block" that she was then building next to the Allis Building (opposite the Old State House) to be "used exclusively for W.C.T.U. work." Notices of meetings in the succeeding years refer to this same address for the WCTU. The Arkansas Woman Suffrage Association also met there often—several notices in the *Arkansas Gazette* tell of upcoming suffrage meetings there.

The address of 313–315 West Markham, therefore, is definitely a key place in the history of civil rights for women in Little Rock. Not only was it where those who specifically wanted votes for women met and discussed the issue, it was also the headquarters of the WCTU for several years, and the WCTU supported women's suffrage from the 1880s.

The McDiarmid Block, also known as the Laclede Hotel, is long gone. It lay directly north of the west side of the U.S. Post Office building.[31] In its place today is a modern office block.

In 1888, Little Rock founded the Arkansas Equal Suffrage Association. The president, Clara McDiarmid, donated meeting rooms in 1889 for women's groups in a new building she had constructed at 313–315 West Markham Street. The offices were formally opened as the headquarters of the WCTU, but the suffrage group also met there regularly. The McDiarmid Block was the small structure to the west of the Allis Block, in the center right of this photograph. (Courtesy of the Butler Center for Arkansas Studies, Little Rock, Arkansas)

Clara McDiarmid, Arkansas's leading suffragist at the end of the nineteenth century. (Courtesy of Mary Mark Ockerbloom, editor, *A Celebration of Women Writers*)

Chapter 4:
Equal Suffrage State Central Committee Offices 1917, 221 West Second Street

In April 1917, the United States joined World War I and threatened to sideline the suffragists' campaign. This brought back bad memories because, after the Civil War, only freedmen—no women—were given the right to vote with the Reconstruction Amendments, even though women had given up their campaign for equal rights for the duration of the war, worked hard for victory, and campaigned for an end to slavery.

Some women refused to repeat that wartime mistake. Alice Paul, the leader of the upstart National Woman's Party (NWP)—which had been pushing for a federal amendment to guarantee women the vote—remembered this vicious betrayal and refused to stop campaigning. Instead, the NWP continued picketing President Wilson outside the White House, inciting the wrath of the public and the administration. Paul and the NWP continued the picketing campaign throughout the war, while the Wilson administration's authoritarian handling of their work finally swung public opinion around to the women's cause.

Meanwhile, at the declaration of war, the largest suffrage organization, the National American Woman Suffrage Association, turned its attention from suffrage to war work. The Arkansas Equal Suffrage State Central Committee, which was formed from the Arkansas Equal Suffrage Association when women won the right to vote in primaries, began to organize suffrage workers in the state for special service during the war. Mrs. O. F. Ellington, chairman of the committee, said: "The work is being done, in fulfillment of the pledge made by suffragists to President Wilson to establish employment bureaus for women, to provide for an increase of the food supply by training women for agricultural work and the elimination of waste, formation of Red Cross units, and to aid in the work of Americanizing the people to prevent trouble from alien sources. Suffragists are being enrolled for service during the war at the State Central Committee headquarters, 427 Southern Trust Building."[32]

The Southern Trust Building opened in 1907 on the southeast corner of Second and Center Streets. At the time, it was Little Rock's tallest building and boasted "the attractions of a summer garden on the roof and a weather observatory."[33] The number 427 in the address may refer to the actual office the women operated in.

When Arkansas suffragists diverted their energies toward war work in 1917, the Equal Suffrage State Central Committee enrolled women for service during the war at its headquarters at 427 Southern Trust Building, now Pyramid Place at 221 West 2nd Street. This historic view—the tall building on the left—is from Louisiana Street looking west. Liberty Hall, where Dr. Anna Howard Shaw spoke, was on the same side of the street opposite the Pulaski County Court House, whose distinctive tower is clearly visible at middle right. Some of the buildings to the east of (in front of) the former Southern Trust Building on the left of the photo still stand. (Courtesy of Ray Hanley)

Alice Paul, leader of the Congressional Union/National Woman's Party, who refused to suspend the women's suffrage campaign in favor of war work in 1917 when President Wilson declared war on Germany. (Courtesy Library of Congress Prints and Photographs Division)

Chapter 5:
The Old State House, 300 West Markham Street

The United States remained in disorder in the aftermath of the Civil War. The major national debate was about rights for freedmen, which the 14th Amendment to the Constitution addressed. In 1866, the Southern states opposed the amendment ferociously. Arkansas rejected it on December 17.

The refusal of the South to ratify an amendment that dealt with citizenship, due process, and equal protection under the law for freed slaves led to the Reconstruction Acts—draconian federal laws which, to bypass this bitter opposition, ignored the legally established governments and imposed military rule in each state until a new civil government was established and the 14th Amendment was ratified.

But rights for freedmen were not the only civil rights in contention at this time: women's rights were also in play. A large number of white women had their first experience as social reformers in abolitionism in the North. They brought this experience to bear when they moved on to issues that directly affected their lives: women's rights. Women first called for suffrage in July 1848 at the Seneca Falls Convention in New York. From then on, they campaigned for the redress of legal inequalities, particularly for married women, and for the vote. Although making some headway with the status of married women, they nevertheless gave up their work to support the Union in the war and redirected their energies toward campaigning for abolition.

The Arkansas State House was one place in the nation where both of these issues emerged. Pursuant to the Reconstruction Acts, in January 1868, delegates from all over Arkansas met in the State House in Little Rock to draw up a new constitution. This was at the same time that the 14th Amendment, guaranteeing citizenship to ex-slaves and enshrining the word "male" in the Constitution for the first time, was proceeding through ratification, to be fully ratified in July 1868. Voting on the new Arkansas Constitution began on March 13 that year.[34] It institutionalized a failure on the part of the delegates in Little Rock. On March 5, Miles Langley, a delegate at the convention from Arkadelphia, had already written about it to Susan B. Anthony, one of the national leaders of the women's suffrage movement:

Dear Friend:

With a sad heart but an approving conscience, I will give you some information relative to the action of our constitutional convention on the franchise question.

The new constitution—a copy of which I send you—makes no difference between men, on account of race or color and contains other excellences; but alas! It fails to guarantee to woman her God-given and well-earned rights of civil and political equality.

I made a motion to insert in the constitution a section to read thus: "All citizens twenty-one years of age, who can read and write the English language, shall be eligible to the elective franchise, and be entitled to equal political and legal rights and privileges." The motion was seconded and I had the floor, but the House became so clamorous that the president could not restore order, and the meeting adjourned with the understanding that I was to occupy the floor the next morning. But the next morning, just as I was about to commence my speech, some of the members tried to "bully" me out of the right to speak on that question. I replied that I had been robbed, shot, and imprisoned for advocating the rights of the slaves, and that I would then and there speak in favor of the rights of women if I had to fight for the right! I then proceeded to present arguments of which I am not ashamed. I was met with ridicule, sarcasm and insult. My ablest opponent, a lawyer, acknowledged in his reply that he could not meet my argument. The motion was laid on the table.

The Democrats are my enemies because I assisted in emancipating the slaves. The Republicans have now become my opponents, because I have made an effort to confer on the women their rights. And even the women themselves fail to sympathize with me.

Very respectfully,
MILES L. LANGLEY.[35]

While some states had previously allowed women to vote, nowhere was there equal suffrage based on gender. The voting rights allowed them to vote only in specific local elections in a couple of states, while the very idea of the right of women to vote was constantly derided. In fact, a few months before the Arkansas convention—in November 1867—and in spite of a fierce campaign, Susan B. Anthony, Elizabeth Cady Stanton, and other suffragists failed to win a proposed constitutional amendment for women's voting rights in Kansas.

Langley's proposal for votes for women in Arkansas arose, therefore, in an atmosphere of hot controversy across the nation about the issue. In this context, his derided 1868 proposal was a missed opportunity for Arkansas to be a trailblazer. If Langley's resolution had been seriously debated and accepted, it would have provided some consolation for the defeat in Kansas the previous year, while Arkansas would have been the first state in the Union in which women had equal suffrage—far ahead of the rest of the country.

Although Wyoming had equal suffrage from 1869, thereby becoming the trailblazing state for votes for women, women won the vote there when Wyoming was admitted to the Union as a *territory* (rather than a state) that year. Yet, it was still the first state with equal suffrage when it was fully admitted to the Union in 1890—more than twenty years after Arkansas could have had equal suffrage.

The men in Arkansas in 1868, like so many men across the nation, were not only prejudiced and short-sighted, but they were also downright insulting to Arkansas women. Those who had crowded the gallery in the legislature to support women's right to vote in the new constitution,[36] would have left disappointed, if not outright angry. If Langley's 1868 proposal had been accepted and become an example for the rest of the nation, it might have prevented the situation whereby all American women had to campaign hard for a further fifty-two years in order to win this most basic civil right. Suffragist Carrie Chapman Catt summarized the problem after women's suffrage was won:

To get the word male...in effect out of the Constitution cost the women of the country fifty-two years of pauseless campaigns thereafter. During that time they were forced to conduct fifty-six campaigns of referenda to male voters; 480 campaigns to urge Legislatures to submit suffrage amendments to voters; 47 campaigns to induce State constitutional conventions to write woman suffrage into State constitutions; 277 campaigns to persuade State party conventions to include woman suffrage planks; 30 campaigns to urge presidential party conventions to adopt woman suffrage planks in party platforms, and 19 campaigns with 19 successive Congresses. Millions of dollars were raised, mainly in small sums, and expended with economic care. Hundreds of women gave the accumulated possibilities of an entire lifetime, thousands gave years of their lives, hundreds of thousands gave constant interest and such aid as they could. It was a continuous, seemingly endless, chain of activity. Young suffragists who helped forge the last links of that chain were not born when it began. Old suffragists who forged the first links were dead when it ended.[37]

It would take fifty more years for women in Arkansas, in just one of these countless campaigns, to win some voting rights. From 1868, the deliberate national exclusion of women from equal suffrage continued in spite of women's fierce opposition to it. The next amendment to the U.S. Constitution, prohibiting the denial of the vote to a citizen based on their "race, color, or previous condition of servitude"—but not on grounds of sex—was introduced in Congress on February 26, 1869. Arkansas ratified this on March 15, 1869, and the amendment achieved national ratification on February 3, 1870, becoming the 15th Amendment to the Constitution.

Equal rights for women came up repeatedly in the Old State House in Arkansas over the succeeding decades. During the 1874 constitutional convention, Judge James Butler urged women's rights, and the new constitution conferred on married women the right to own property that "may be devised, bequeathed, or conveyed by her the same as if she were a single woman."[38] Later laws for the rights of married women further improved their legal status, but "[t]he Supreme Court took a dim view of the liberation of women and emasculated the law in a number of late 19th century court decisions."[39] At that time, the Old State House was the home of the Supreme Court of Arkansas, where these decisions were handed down. Yet Arkansas was only reflecting much of what was going on at the national level. Every attempt that women made in the Northeast and in Missouri to win women the right to vote through court cases that could go to the Supreme Court failed for various reasons.[40]

The Old State House played a role in suffrage again in 1891 when one legislator, playing the "race card," attempted to enfranchise white women only. The move, which would have been unconstitutional, failed. The Old State House was center stage again in 1893 when the Arkansas Woman Suffrage Association held its third annual convention in the Hall of Representatives on April 29. The participants passed the following resolution: "That we use our influence as an organization and individually against the election to offices of public trust any man opposed to equal suffrage under the law."[41]

In January 1911, the center of state government moved to the new State Capitol. As a result of public protest, much of it from women, the Old State House was preserved and in 1914, it became once again the center of Arkansas women's campaign for the vote.

The National American Woman Suffrage Association (NAWSA)—an amalgamation of two large suffrage organizations from the nineteenth century—had pursued a policy for many years of promoting suffrage through the states, but by the general election of 1912, women had won equal voting rights in only nine states. Alice Paul and Lucy Burns—two much younger women than those in the NAWSA—began working from the start of 1913 for a federal amendment, initially through the NAWSA. Later, when the NAWSA disagreed with Paul's tactics, her group pursued the federal amendment independently as the Congressional Union and then the National Woman's Party.

In January 1914, Paul called for nationwide suffrage days on May 2 in every state. These meetings were called to pass resolutions and deliver them to Washington DC in a huge rally there on May 9. Paul's group immediately began to organize the meetings nationally, harnessing the network of local branches of the NAWSA. Meanwhile, as usual, Susan B. Anthony's 1878 proposal for a federal amendment for votes for women was introduced in Congress, and the NAWSA—disagreeing with Paul's group's tactics—lobbied Congress to vote on it for the first time, even though support was not there. It was defeated in March

1914. Now Paul's call for "coast-to-coast demonstrations" on May 2, 1914, took on new import. Arkansas women's part in this national rally took place on that day on the grounds of the Old State House, a week before women from all over the country gathered in Washington DC on May 9 to lobby Congress for votes for women.[42]

In 1916, in the very location where suffrage was laughed down thirty-six years before, officers of the newly formed Arkansas branch of the Congressional Union assembled at the doorway to display the Great Demand Banner and convey the challenge of the federal amendment suffrage cause.[43]

Suffrage Day at the Old State House, May 1914. The Old State House was decked out in suffrage colors—here the tricolor purple, white, and gold that Alice Paul introduced to the NAWSA in 1913 when spearheading the National Congressional Committee for a Constitutional Amendment. Later these became the identifying colors of Paul's National Woman's Party. The NAWSA's own color was sunflower gold and sometimes black. (Courtesy of the Arkansas History Commission, Little Rock, Arkansas)

Chapter 6:
Capital Theater—Susan B. Anthony Speaks, 200 Block, West Markham Street (south side)

"Miss Anthony," read the headline in the newspaper in Little Rock one day in February 1889. In the report that followed, it stated: "A very fair audience heard Miss Susan B. Anthony's lecture upon 'Woman Suffrage' at the Capital Theater last night and the marked attention of her listeners was a sufficient voucher for the entertaining character of her remarks. She was introduced to the audience by Governor J. P. Eagle."[44]

Susan B. Anthony was the pre-eminent suffragist in the United States. She came to Little Rock a year after Clara McDiarmid and thirteen other women formed the Arkansas Equal Suffrage Association (AESA). Although there is no documentary evidence, it is reasonable to assume from the timing that Anthony's visit was linked to the formation of that organization in 1888. Today, the Stephens Building at 111 Center Street incorporates its former location.

It is equally reasonable to assume by the tone of the article in the *Gazette* that the writer was a man. He continued his report: "It is a truth that suffrage is a boon not desired by a very heavy majority of the most refined and intelligent women of the country. If it were so, the results for which the lecturer has given her life's energies would doubtless be very easy of accomplishment. It is sufficient to say further that if woman desired this one privilege she would obtain it by the same means which she uses in gaining from men the satisfaction of her every other want."

The writer was correct that only a minority of women in the United States actively professed to wanting the right to vote, but minority status did not make the aspiration invalid. A majority of women actively seeking the right to vote would not necessarily make it "very easy of accomplishment" either. That assertion flew in the face of facts. In the late 1880s, the struggle for votes for women was already more than forty years old. Twenty years earlier, during Reconstruction, congressmen had resolutely refused to extend the vote to women at a most propitious time in the country's history for doing so. The *Gazette* writer, who was strong on "facts," also failed to consider the further fact that judges, and justices of the Supreme Court, were exclusively male—and they had in the 1870s judged against the plaintiffs and petitioners in cases that women brought before them to try to secure the vote. He did not consider either that all the legislators were male, and that most of them were against votes for women. Even thirty years after Anthony's visit to Little Rock, ratification of the 19th Amendment by which women won the vote squeaked through the 36th state—Tennessee—by just one vote.

Anthony had come to women's suffrage upon leaving teaching. Her first foray into reform was the campaign for temperance, which sought to make alcohol illegal to prevent drunken husbands from abusing their families and making them destitute. Anthony began speaking publicly for temperance in 1849 and found her life's work in suffrage in 1852. Anthony also supported abolition of slavery, and her drive and effectiveness soon encouraged abolitionist leaders to recruit her as a speaker and organizer in 1856.[45] As she had no independent income, the job gave her the means to make her living in working for reform. Later, during the Civil War, she and her colleague Elizabeth Cady Stanton also spearheaded a huge petition campaign for full emancipation after they were shocked to discover the limited nature of President Lincoln's 1863 Emancipation Proclamation. That petition prompted the introduction of the 13th Amendment.

After the Civil War, when women's rights were ignored in spite of all they had done for the war and for the abolition of slavery, Anthony campaigned against the 14th and 15th Amendments, which guaranteed the vote only to men. She did so not because she was racist, as critics asserted—her stand for abolition negates that argument—but because the amendments excluded women. Specifically, the 14th Amendment put the word "male" into the Constitution for the first time, and she knew that if ratified, it would take generations to remove it. The history of women's suffrage proves she was right. So much for the observation that votes for women was "very easy of accomplishment."[46]

Anthony is the leading suffragist who campaigned for a federal amendment to ban discrimination in voting on account of sex, just as discrimination against "race, color or previous condition of servitude" had been banned by the 15th Amendment. Although it was mooted first during the Reconstruction controversies, a sympathetic congressman finally introduced Anthony's proposal in January 1878. This was nearly three years after civil disobedience by women had failed miserably—both with the trial and illegal conviction of Anthony herself for voting in the presidential election of 1872, and with the Supreme Court judgment in 1875 that declared that although women were citizens, citizenship did not confer any right to vote, so sex discrimination in voting was not banned.[47] In the resoluteness of her resistance, Anthony was the precursor of Alice Paul and her colleagues in the twentieth century. Paul and the National Woman's Party in 1916 christened what became the 19th Amendment "the Susan B. Anthony Amendment" to distinguish it from another amendment that the older suffrage organization, the NAWSA, had lobbied for in 1914 in an attempt to discredit Paul and her supporters for their ground-breaking tactics.

After Anthony's talk in Little Rock in 1889, the *Woman's Chronicle* commented: "Miss Anthony proved very conclusively to her audience…that what women needed was the ballot. She laid a broad solid foundation…by illustrations of what the franchise had done for the working man of other countries and what it has done for the negro at home. On this foundation she built step by step such a pyramid of statistics, principles and ideas as so one could undermine.[48]

Anthony again delivered a lecture at the Capital Theater on February 24, this time on temperance under the auspices of the Woman's Christian Temperance Union (WCTU).[49] Originally scheduled to take place in the Christian Church, public demand presumably prompted the change.[50] Possibly instrumental in arranging this visit by Susan B. Anthony to Arkansas—she spoke in Fort Smith, Hot Springs, and Helena—was Clara McDiarmid, who was a member of the Christian Church,[51] had been involved with temperance for several years, and had become a founding member and first president of the Arkansas Equal Suffrage Association in February 1888.[52] She exemplified the close link between suffrage and temperance in Little Rock.

The Little Rock WCTU was established in the city in 1879.[53] When exactly McDiarmid joined is unknown but in February 1888, she was a local officer and became an officer in the state organization that June.[54]

In February 1889, Susan B. Anthony came to Little Rock and spoke on suffrage in the Capital Theater. The following Sunday, she spoke on temperance. This advertisement of the week before advertised Susan B. Anthony's upcoming visit to the city. The Capital Theater was in the block which the Stephens Building now occupies. (Source: Woman's Chronicle, *February 5, 1889, Arkansas History Commission)*

AMUSEMENTS.

CAPITAL THEATER.

W. O. THOMAS, MANAGER.

ONE NIGHT ONLY.

Thursday, February 21,

The World Famous

SUSAN B. ANTHONY

Will Lecture On

What Woman

Wants !

Miss Anthony's First Visit

SOUTH.

PRICES: 75c and 50c.

Sale of seats commence Tuesday, February 19, at box office.

Susan B. Anthony, one of the two leaders of the National Woman Suffrage Association, was the preeminent suffragist in the United States when she visited Little Rock in 1889. The National Woman's Party dedicated the 19th Amendment to her in 1914. (Source: Author collection, *History of Woman Suffrage*, Vol. IV)

Chapter 7:
Marion Hotel, 200 Block, West Markham Street (north side)

ittle Rock's Marion Hotel was almost the headquarters of women's suffrage from 1911 to 1920. It appears in news stories more than any other as a place where suffragists stayed and held meetings while campaigning for votes for women. In March 1911, the *Arkansas Gazette* reported:

> Overcome by feminine attractiveness and overpowered by forceful argument, the Constitutional Committee of the house, known as the "Old Guard" went down to defeat from the Woman's Political Equality League and with meekly bowed heads and subdued voices voted that the bill proposing an amendment to the constitution to give the women a right to vote be recommended favorable to the house. From the first round until the last the Constitutional Committee was outmatched by eloquent suffragists with the result that the league won the first battle in its effort to gain the ballot for Arkansas women.
>
> The committee from the league had an engagement with the Constitutional Committee at 4:30 o'clock in the banquet hall of the Hotel Marion and that hour all the members of the committee were on hand. When the Constitutional Committee reached the Hotel Marion after the house had adjourned several false starts were made to face the assembled women.[55]

The bill referred to was for a state constitutional amendment to allow women twenty-one years or older to vote. It was introduced on January 20, 1911, but nothing reports what triggered this bill. A letter received by young society matron Adolphine Fletcher Terry in April 1910 seems to indicate, however, that some women in Little Rock were interested in suffrage at the time; they may have been behind the move.

The letter refers to a request that Terry made to Senator James P. Clarke's office asking for a sympathetic hearing "to the representatives of the equal suffrage society" when they were in Washington DC. It is not known what society this might have been.[56] Her sister may have been involved. Terry later reported that her sister Mary Fletcher, who, like Adolphine, had attended Vassar (but a decade later), had participated in a famous suffrage meeting held in a cemetery by soon-to-be-memorable National Woman's Party (NWP) leader Inez Milholland in defiance of the college president's bans.[57] This may be a link to the missing back story to the January 1911 proposed amendment. In February 1911, in fact, Mary Fletcher would publicly become a Little Rock suffragist as the first president of the newly founded Political Equality League of Little Rock. Through Fletcher, therefore—and likely also through several other women, though at present nameless—a growing interest in suffrage may have taken hold in Little Rock around 1910, prompting the 1911 proposed constitutional amendment.

A local development in Arkansas would have formed part of a national trend, for, since 1907, American women—increasingly influenced by the tactics of British suffragists to the extent of taking to the streets to promote suffrage—had started attempting suffrage parades, only to be thwarted by authorities. Finally, after some successful parades in western states, on May 21, 1910, the first large one was held on the East Coast in New York when Harriet Stanton Blatch's Equality League of Self-Supporting Women and more than 400 supporters headed down Fifth Avenue to a mass meeting in Union Square, displaying British-style protest and demand banners. Such parades became annual events.[58] The British influence in this parade was direct, for soon-to-be notorious Alice Paul had spoken at Blatch's invitation in New York's Cooper Union three months before on her return to the United States after being force-fed in an English prison for fighting for the cause.[59]

The result of the 1911 Marion Hotel meeting that the *Gazette* reported on in March—during which several women spoke—was that the committee recommended a favorable vote in the House. The bill, however, failed.

The Marion Hotel opened in 1907 to meet the demand for high-class hotel accommodations in Little Rock. Owner Herman Kahn named it after his wife, Marion.[60] This hotel was a twin to one in Alexandria, Louisiana. Photographs indicate that it was also very much like the 1913 Hotel Pines on Pine Bluff's Main Street, still extant but sadly dilapidated.[61] Little Rock's version is long gone—the Little Rock Marriott, formerly the Peabody, takes its place.

The 1911 meeting is only the first time the hotel features in the women's suffrage movement in Arkansas. In 1914, it was the scene of a conference called by the Little Rock and Hot Springs Political Equality Leagues "for the purpose of devising ways and means of forming a State association....In October the State Woman Suffrage Association was formed in Little Rock at Hotel Marion."[62]

In 1916, the Marion Hotel took center stage again:

> At 2:30 o'clock this afternoon a Congressional Union conference will be held at the Hotel Marion, at which an Arkansas committee of the union will be appointed to assist in the fight to secure an amendment to the constitution of the United States giving women the right to vote. At the meeting Miss Alice Paul of Washington, chairman of the Congressional Union, will explain the work of the union, tell of the need of the aid of Arkansas women, and urge them to help secure the support of Arkansas senators and representatives in Congress.
> Mrs. David Terry [Adolphine Fletcher Terry] will preside...Miss Mabel Vernon of Washington, a member of the union, will give a short address.[63]

"[M]eetings were held afternoon and night at the convention hall in the Hotel Marion," it was reported the next day. The meetings were successful, with an Arkansas chapter of the Congressional Union (later the National Woman's Party) established with "Mrs. Edward M. Jarrett elected chairman of the Executive Committee for Arkansas....Mrs. David D. Terry was elected a member of the National Advisory Board of the union and ex-officio member of the Executive Committee for Arkansas."

The meetings—in Little Rock, Pine Bluff, and Hot Springs—collected a total of $530 in funds for the national campaign for a federal amendment.[64] The *Arkansas Democrat*'s much shorter report stated that $350 had been subscribed for the federal amendment work.[65] Alice Paul and Mabel Vernon may have stayed at the hotel during their visit to Little Rock.

That April, hard on Alice Paul's heels, Carrie Chapman Catt, the new president of the National American Woman Suffrage Association (NAWSA), appeared in Little Rock for a conference, and her words then showed that the NAWSA had started buying into the NWP federal suffrage amendment campaign, although not completely. Asked whether the approach to women's suffrage should be through a national amendment or state-by-state, Catt said: "Both are the best. We must knock at every door that we see open. It may come, state by state. And yet I think also that it is not so far in the future before we shall see a national amendment to our constitution."[66]

Catt was specifically laying claim here for NAWSA to the federal women's suffrage amendment policy in an attempt to undermine its identification in the public mind with Alice Paul and the Congressional Union. Catt's mentor, Susan B. Anthony, had worked for the introduction of a federal women's suffrage amendment in Congress in 1878. To the extent that the NAWSA emerged out of a union between Anthony's radical organization (the National Woman Suffrage Association) and a more conservative organization (the American Woman Suffrage Association) in 1890, Catt's claim was correct.

The NAWSA, however, by concentrating on the state-by-state policy almost since the time of the union of the two national suffrage organizations, had ignored Anthony's legacy. Even when Paul and her colleagues had taken up the federal amendment through the NAWSA's Congressional Committee in 1913, Paul's introduction of "unwomanly" tactics had led to her withdrawal—or expulsion—from the NAWSA. Paul's own Congressional Union (later the NWP) took up the pursuit of the federal amendment with increasingly assertive tactics. By 1916, Paul and her workers had introduced new energy into the struggle for women's suffrage, and when she appeared in Little Rock and spoke at the Marion Hotel in January 1916, she had introduced a new factor into Little Rock suffrage work, which Catt needed to counter.

The Marion Hotel featured again in women's suffrage in March 1917—this time as the scene of a significant triumph on the path toward suffrage in Arkansas. The *Arkansas Gazette* stated: "Passage of the Riggs bill permitting women to vote in primaries in Arkansas was celebrated with great enthusiasm at a suffrage mass meeting at the Hotel Marion last night. The climax was reached when Governor [Charles] Brough signed the bill at the end of his stirring address on woman suffrage. The big convention hall was filled to overflowing."[67]

Arkansas's suffragists had campaigned for the bill granting women the right to vote in primaries following the introduction of the NAWSA's "Winning Plan" to get whatever suffrage was possible—and primary suffrage was more possible than equal suffrage because the former required only an act of the Arkansas assembly. The *Gazette* reported that the mass meeting during which Governor Brough signed the bill was originally planned for "one of the rooms at the Pulaski county court house, but the attendance...which exceeded expectation, caused the promoters to seek a larger auditorium."[68] The historic court house, therefore, narrowly missed being a location of suffrage activity.

Again in 1917, on November 9, Jane Pincus arrived in Little Rock and stayed at the Marion Hotel, preparing the way for Mabel Vernon's visit ten days later on her latest campaign for the NWP. Her arrival and the impending arrival of Mabel Vernon upset many Arkansas suffrage women because of differences of opinion about the continuation of the suffrage campaign and tactics when the nation was fighting in World War I.

Since January 1917, the NWP had been increasing the pressure by picketing the White House for presidential support for a federal amendment for votes for women. At the time of the vote for war in April of that year, Alice Paul had declared that she would not stop the picketing. Women had learned a hard lesson with the Civil War when they had suspended their work for women's rights in 1861, believing reforms to benefit themselves would follow their fulfillment of their patriotic duty. But the Reconstruction Amendments had guaranteed the right to vote only to men—and specified males in the Constitution for the first time in the nation's history. With such a betrayal of women more than fifty years before, Paul refused to risk the same again. In fact, by keeping up the pressure, they could now demand that President Woodrow Wilson's call for a suffrage amendment be considered a war measure. It was good thinking, for war measures generally pass through both houses of congress with little opposition.

Paul and the NWP, however, found themselves facing criticism and mounting opposition when they continued their picketing. In July 1917, arrests of the picketers—known as the Silent Sentinels—began. These arrests were later declared unconstitutional, but, in the meantime, the NWP continued its campaign. Attacks both by the public and the authorities increased in ferocity and, to highlight the hypocrisy of President Wilson, who was talking about promoting and defending democracy abroad while treating U.S. citizens violently at home, some of the women went on hunger strike.

By November 1917, Alice Paul was in prison and being force-fed, and many other White House picketers were being arrested daily when Jane Pincus and Mabel Vernon—themselves picketers and suffrage prisoners—came to Little Rock in the middle of the month. The behavior of Little Rock's women now reflected exactly what was happening at the national level. Paul's emissaries faced what the newspapers called a "Jack Frost" reception of the suffragists of Little Rock who supported only the tactics of the NAWSA, which had encouraged its members to turn from campaigning to war work.[69]

November 1917 was a busy month for suffragists in the state and for the Marion Hotel. On Friday, November 16, Arkansas suffragists hosted a "New York Victory" luncheon there for Mrs. T. T. Cotnam of the local NAWSA-affiliated group. Cotnam, Gertrude Watkins, and Josephine Miller had worked around New York to help win suffrage there.[70] Then, when Mabel Vernon arrived in Little Rock two days later on November 18, the Marion was her base for planning meetings and contacting local suffrage leaders such as Adolphine Fletcher Terry, Mrs. John P. Almand, Mrs. DeMatt Henderson, Mrs. L. B. Leigh, and others "to explain the campaign which…must be conducted during the first two weeks of Congress to assure adoption of the federal amendment this session."[71]

Less than two years later, the NWP's tactics finally paid off. In July 1919, the evening before the special session of the state legislature which ratified the Susan B. Anthony Amendment, the Marion Hotel was the scene of meetings between "the leading members of the Central Committee of the suffrage organizations...and the [legislators].[72] The next day, the Central Committee hosted a luncheon at the Marion Hotel for Governor Brough and members of the legislature for their return to Little Rock to ratify the 19th Amendment, which they duly did on July 28, 1919.[73]

A faint echo of all this activity for votes for women also took place in the Marion Hotel in 1966, when a testimonial dinner was held to honor the work of Adolphine Fletcher Terry for her untiring efforts during the desegregation crisis in Little Rock in the late 1950s. Terry had been a prime mover and shaker behind the Women's Emergency Committee to Open Our Schools, formed to support reopening the schools under the district's desegregation plan.

One item read out to the audience during the event was a "note... from Mrs. Fred I. Brown, who observed in it that she and Mrs. Terry had marched together years ago, carrying banners demanding equal rights for women. 'Is Josephine here?' Mrs. Terry asked. When Mrs. Brown identified herself in the audience, the venerable lady cracked, 'We still haven't got them!'"[74] Mrs. Brown was the Josephine Miller who campaigned in Arkansas, as well as in New York in 1917.[75]

While treatments of Adolphine Fletcher Terry mention her work for votes for women in passing, none of them communicate the strength of Terry's background in women's rights—a background that contributed to the power of her stand on desegregation. Terry may have worked with Little Rock's mainstream suffrage organizations, but she also aligned herself with Alice Paul and the NWP—the group whose work pushed the votes-for-women campaign forward at a breakneck pace. Without that campaign, votes for female U.S. citizens very likely would not have become a reality in 1920. Terry stuck with the NWP through the promulgation of the 19th Amendment. Terry's awareness of, and obvious interest in, women's rights shines through this protest that occurred during the dinner held to honor all her other work.

Marion Hotel, Little Rock, Ark.

Opened in 1907 and named after the owner's wife, Little Rock's Marion Hotel was arguably the headquarters of women's suffrage from 1911 to 1920, hosting both local suffragist rallies and meetings of prominent national suffragists. The Marion was located where the Little Rock Marriott, previously the Peabody, now stands.

The main lobby of the Marion Hotel would have seen Alice Paul and Carrie Chapman Catt and their followers milling around or having tea and planning strategy, for Paul and Catt stayed and held meetings here during the suffrage campaign. Arkansas suffragists also held many a rally here. Its "big convention hall was filled to overflowing" when Governor Brough signed the just-passed Riggs Bill, which secured Arkansas women the right to vote in primary elections in March 1917. (Both photos courtesy of the Butler Center for Arkansas Studies, Little Rock)

Alice Paul was the twenty-six-year-old leader who from 1913 spearheaded the innovative political campaign that ultimately won women the vote. Paul visited Little Rock in January 1916, held meetings at the Marion Hotel, and likely stayed there while rallying Arkansas women for a local branch of the Congressional Union/National Woman's Party. Late in 1917, the non-violent tactics she used to win the vote brought public opprobrium on her head. Here her hunger strike makes headlines in Little Rock.
(Source: *Arkansas Gazette*, November 7, 1917, 5)

Suffragette Leader Who Threatens to Starve Self

MISS ALICE PAUL

ALICE PAUL GOES ON HUNGER STRIKE

Says She Will Kill Herself Unless Better Food Is Given Suffragette Prisoners.

MISS LULA SCRUGGS.

After women won the vote in primary elections, Lula Scruggs, a North Little Rock suffrage leader, alerted women to the state and local laws and regulations that restricted voting. Women's poll tax had to be paid and the receipt correctly completed in order to ensure they would not be disqualified in the primaries. (Source: Arkansas Gazette, April 9, 1917)

Chapter 8:
The Suffragists "At Home" at the Capital Hotel, 113–123 West Markham Street

What is known today as the Capital Hotel—it started out as an office building in the 1870s—played a role in the history of woman suffrage.

Its first role was during the visit of Carrie Chapman Catt to the city in May 1900. Catt's suffrage lineage was impressive. Only that February, she had taken over leadership of the National American Woman Suffrage Association (NAWSA) from Susan B. Anthony, the nineteenth century's iconic suffragist. As new president of the NAWSA, Catt "was making a tour of the south in the interest of the movement." The votes for the women's suffrage movement had begun in the New England states—only late in the century did Southern women begin to take part. Catt "will deliver a free lecture tonight at the Y.M.C.A. hall on Eighth and Main streets," the *Arkansas Democrat* reported.[76] The same paper described her the next day as "a most entertaining and forceful speaker" and added: "This afternoon in the parlors of the Capital Hotel, Mrs. Catt will hold an informal reception at which time she hopes to meet the ladies of Little Rock. This will be from 3 to 5 o'clock."[77]

With such a venue for her "informal reception," it is more than likely that Catt also stayed at the hotel during her quick visit to Little Rock. The *Democrat* in the same report also announced that Catt would give a second lecture in the chapel of the First Methodist Episcopal Church South, and again it would be open to all. Catt, therefore, replicated what had happened eleven years before during Susan B. Anthony's visit when a second lecture was arranged hurriedly because of the popularity and success of the speaker. This indicates the interest in the city for the subject and such national speakers.

More than a decade later, the Capital Hotel played another part in suffrage on the National Suffrage Day of 1914, when, after a rally at the Old State House, Little Rock's supporters of votes for women gathered for a luncheon in the Capital Hotel. It was a momentous occasion, as reported by the *Arkansas Gazette*:

> At 1:30 o'clock this afternoon the suffragettes and "votes for women" sympathizers will enjoy an elaborate luncheon at the New Capital hotel. Miss Julia Warner will preside as toastmistress and toasts will be responded to by leading suffragists from all over the state. A large number of men identified with the cause of woman's suffrage, also will respond to toasts at the luncheon.[78]
>
> The old statehouse was decorated with the national emblem and the colors of the suffrage organizations, white and yellow. The banquet hall at the New Capital was also similarly decorated, the handiwork of Mrs. Leonard Drennan and Mrs. S.S. Wassell....The guests assembled in the large banquet hall at the New Capital hotel where luncheon was served in courses....200 were served at the luncheon....The luncheon committee was composed of Mrs. Clarence E. Rose, Miss Gertrude Watkins, Miss Louisa Gibson, Miss Frances Edmondson and Miss Josephine Miller...
>
> The luncheon at the New Capital hotel, in charge of Mrs. George B. Cunningham, was one of the delightful features of the day's celebration. Miss Julia Warner, versatile in wit and humor, and enthusiastic in the cause, which apparently "lacked no resistance" yesterday, was the mistress of the situation from beginning to end, her pleasant remarks and appropriate words employed in the introduction of speakers, evoking hearty rounds of applause.[79]

The same report listed other speakers and concluded: "Music by an orchestra was furnished during the progress of the luncheon, and a delightful viola solo was rendered by Mrs. Adele Johnson of Hot Springs, accompanied by Miss Josephine Miller."[80]

Little Rock's Capital Hotel has seen such famous figures as General Ulysses S. Grant strolling through its lobby. It became the stage for suffrage activity when the new president of the National American Woman Suffrage Association, Carrie Chapman Catt, stayed in April 1900 and held informal receptions there. (Courtesy of the Butler Center for Arkansas Studies, Little Rock, Arkansas)

Josephine Miller, later Mrs. Fred I. Brown, delivered one of the many five-minute speeches during the 1914 suffrage rally at the Old State House and performed during the reception at the Capital Hotel. In 1916, she joined the Congressional Union and later became a national organizer for the NAWSA. (Courtesy of the Josephine Miller Brown Family Archives)

Gertrude Watkins was an organizer of the 1914 post-rally Suffrage Day luncheon at the Capital Hotel. In 1916, she joined the Congressional Union and later became a national organizer for the NAWSA. (Courtesy of the Dr. Claibourne and Mrs. Mildred Farley Watkins Family Collection)

Chapter 9:
The **Woman's Chronicle,**
122 West Second Street

n March 1888, Catherine Campbell Cuningham,[81] Mary Burt Brooks, and Haryot Holt Cahoon launched the *Woman's Chronicle*. The first issue does not refer to the founding of the Arkansas Equal Suffrage Association (AESA) the previous month, but the newspaper's establishment followed hard on the heels of the creation of the AESA. It is likely that the founding meeting discussed the loss of the *Southern Ladies' Journal* the previous year and the need for a new publication. Cuningham, Brooks, and Cahoon seem to have begun immediately to create a new publication. It is also likely that the meeting that founded the AESA had been called by women interested in women's concerns to deal with two pressing issues: the lack of their own newspaper and the cause of women's suffrage. The existence and stance of the *Chronicle* reflect these concerns.

A year later, Ida Joe Brooks described the meeting that founded the AESA. "Three of the number were less than twenty-one years of age, and five were not residents of the city…it was not a formidable party," she said.[82] She added, "We have at present sixty-seven members of our local society."

The earliest reference to the *Chronicle*'s office location was in the March 3, 1888, issue, where it was stated to be at the "corner Main and Second Streets, over Bolling & Badgett's drug store." Within months, however, it was reported that "the office of WOMAN'S CHRONICLE [was] moved, to the new Reaves building, corner of Second and Louisiana streets, on the second floor."[83] The Reaves Building occupied the northeast corner of Second and Louisiana, which today is a parking lot for the Capital Hotel. The address in those days was listed as 122 West 2nd Street.[84] Susan B. Anthony visited the *Chronicle*'s offices during her trip to Little Rock in February 1889, a visit which the staff there referred to as "a pleasant call."[85]

Throughout its five years of publication, the *Woman's Chronicle* covered women's suffrage locally, statewide, and nationally. It became the official publication of the Woman's Christian Temperance Union (WCTU) and reported on other women's organizations, such as the Children's Home, the Woman's Exchange, the Industrial Home, and the Old Ladies' Home. It also covered social activities extensively and is therefore a valuable source of tidbits of the history of individual women between 1888 and 1893. The *Chronicle* delivered its latest edition every week to all members of the General Assembly to inform them of women's concerns.

When the *Chronicle* folded in 1893 because of founder Catherine Cuningham's illness, the Arkansas Woman Suffrage Association passed a resolution at its annual meeting: "That we deplore the suspension of the *Chronicle*, our state organ, and hope it may be resumed at an early date."[86]

Sadly, both for the suffrage and other women's organizations of the time, as well as for the historical record, the wish expressed in the resolution was not realized.

In March 1888, three Little Rock women launched the Woman's Chronicle, which advocated for votes for women. With its first offices at Main and Second Streets over Bolling & Badgett's drugstore, it soon moved upstairs in the new Reaves building at 122 West 2nd Street, on the northeast corner of the intersection with Louisiana. Susan B. Anthony visited the offices when in Little Rock in February 1889. Although an excellent paper, the Chronicle never made money and folded in 1894 when one of its founders became ill. (Courtesy of Ray Hanley)

The masthead of the Woman's Chronicle, which first appeared in March 1888 and ceased publication in 1893. (Courtesy of the Arkansas History Commission, Little Rock, Arkansas)

The former location of the offices of the Woman's Chronicle *today serves as a parking lot for the Capital Hotel.* (Photo by Ron Davis, 2010)

Chapter 10:
Old City Hall, 120–122 West Markham Street

n January 1870, the *Arkansas Gazette* reported on a talk given in Little Rock on a Monday at what was then City Hall at 120–122 West Markham Street. "No similar event, worthy of mention, has ever before occurred in this city," the writer commented.

The unique event was the appearance in town of Phoebe Couzins to deliver an address "on the right of women to exercise, and the duty of men to concede to her, the rights of franchise."[87]

Couzins was from a prominent family of activist reformers from St. Louis, Missouri. An activist herself during her twenties, she realized that a legal education was important for women, and she began studies in 1868 at what was then the St. Louis School of Law. In 1871, she was the first woman to graduate from the school, the first female law graduate in Missouri, and only the third female law graduate in the United States.[88]

Couzins's appearance in Little Rock, therefore, occurred when she was a law student of about thirty years old. The *Gazette* noted that "about a hundred and fifty persons, ladies and gentlemen, composing a very select audience [were] present to hear the address." Then it devoted the rest of a comparatively long newspaper paragraph for the time to commenting on the "young lady's" appearance, demeanor, and the clothes she wore, as if she were a child or at most a teenager. The third paragraph of the report continued with a cursory summary of the content of her talk and finished with a put-down of her position.

Except for recording that the event took place, the report from Arkansas's newspaper of record contains little useful information about what Couzins might actually have said in favor of suffrage. There is, however, in Couzins's family archives, "an unidentified newspaper clipping" from 1871 of *A Speech By The Lady Bachelor At Law* which contains what she might have said in Little Rock in 1870. It argues that women's acceptance of the notion of women as the fairer and weaker sex, fit only for the private sphere, does not make them victims; instead, it is a sign of abdicating responsibility and potential power, with deleterious effects upon society:

> [W]oman should hasten to repair her ignorance of [the country's] laws and needs, by a thorough knowledge and acquaintance of those which govern her and affect her humanity. Her moral and political irresponsibility seems one; she can no longer retain the lily's passive state in the world's field of action; henceforth, she must be a helper, not an idler; and, believing this, I am glad to welcome any and all movements which tend to lift woman out of her narrow, traditional life, and place her upon her feet, where she may think and act for herself. Hitherto, the doctrine of self-reliance, self-culture, personal responsibility, has never been taught to woman; she has been regarded as created for man's self-love, alone; with no soul to feel, no mind to expand, no brain to weigh argument, no individual accountability to render her Maker, and thus the race has slowly, painfully climbed the heights of progress, dragging a dead weight, securely manacled at the feet and wrists, which its own hands have forged. This inert mass now threatens death and destruction unless related from bondage. Woman's irresponsibility and man's culpably negligence is working ruin to our social and political fabric; and, unless some power can galvanize the slumbering virtue of this people into new life, we, as nation, are doomed to irresistible disaster.

Phoebe Couzins later became one of the leading suffragists in the nineteenth century, along with Susan B. Anthony and Elizabeth Cady Stanton. She became so prominent that her image appears as the frontispiece in the third volume of Anthony and Stanton's *History of Woman Suffrage*. She reappeared in Arkansas early in the 1880s, in Eureka Springs, as a co-founder along with Lizzie Dorman Fyler of the state's first women's suffrage organization.[89] Later in life, Couzins disavowed the early stand she had taken and expressed in Little Rock, especially for women's right to vote, alienating many by her behavior. She died in poverty in 1913.[90]

The year Couzins spoke in Little Rock, City Hall was located on West Markham Street. The 1876 Directory describes it as at the "north side of Markham, west of Main." The 1878 City Directory lists the address at 120–122 West Markham.

Little Rock's Old City Hall was located at 120–122 West Markham Street when Phoebe Couzins called for votes for women there in January 1870—less than two years after delegates derided votes for women at the Constitutional Convention. This 1950s image shows its incarnation long after Old City Hall was replaced by the current City Hall. It was in the block opposite the Capital Hotel at the foot of Main, where today's Statehouse Convention Center now stands. (Courtesy of the Arkansas History Commission, Little Rock, Arkansas)

Phoebe Couzins's talk when she spoke in Old City Hall in January 1870 on votes for women made news in the Arkansas Gazette. *She later helped Lizzie D. Fyler to create the state's first suffrage organization, located in Eureka Springs, and became almost as famous as suffragist Susan B. Anthony. (Source: Author collection,* History of Woman Suffrage, *Vol. III)*

Chapter 11:
Woman's Christian Temperance Union, 106 East Markham Street

In June 1888, a notice appeared in the "Some Local Gleanings" column of Little Rock's groundbreaking Southern women's newspaper, the *Woman's Chronicle*, which was founded in March of that year.

The notice states that the Little Rock Woman's Christian Temperance Union (WCTU) "will give a reception at state headquarters, 106 E Markham street (second floor), to state officers and all others who incline to come, from 5 to 10 p.m., Thursday, 21st inst. Refreshments will be served, and any donations of a character to furnish either a parlor or dining-room will be gladly received."

The call for donations of furnishings must have paid off, for on July 14, 1888, a letter appeared in the city's venerable newspaper, the *Arkansas Gazette*, founded in 1819.

> To the Editor of the *Gazette*:
>
> LITTLE ROCK, July 11.—I wish to call the attention of the good people of Little Rock to the fact that the State W.C.T.U. have opened headquarters at 106 ½ East Markham, that we have established a lunch-room at the same place, where we shall be pleased to see our friends at lunch hours, except mornings. Iced milk and tea, hot coffee, sandwiches, etc. We do not give free lunch, but think our charges, 15 cents, very reasonable.
>
> T.A. DUNLAP,
> State Cor. Sec. W.C.T.U.[91]

The national WCTU was founded in 1874. The Little Rock organization followed in 1879. The archival records of the meetings of the Little

Rock group seem to begin only in January 1889, but from 1881, it had been meeting "every Tuesday in the home of William H. Field at 811 Scott Street." It had twenty-nine members, and ultimately the Little Rock organization became one of the most active and influential in the nation.[92]

The *Woman's Chronicle* also reports other WCTU meetings held in the Presbyterian Chapel, at "the First Presbyterian Church, corner of Scott and Fifth streets," and at the YMCA rooms, with an election meeting held at the YMCA rooms on February 9, 1888.[93] It is not stated clearly whether these meetings were state or Little Rock meetings, but, as separate news stories refer to state meetings, it may be inferred that some of these meetings were local branch meetings.

Temperance and suffrage had something to offer each other. If women had the vote, they could vote for temperance. In return, temperance's national grassroots network offered suffrage both an organizational example and potential supporters. In fact, in 1875, Susan B. Anthony allowed the union of the work of the WCTU and the Women's New York State Temperance Society, which she had helped organize in 1851, because of the potential synergy between her work and the temperance goals.[94]

In Little Rock, local women were often members of both the WCTU and the Arkansas Woman Suffrage Association after the founding of the latter in early 1888, including WCTU officer and later suffragist Fannie Chunn.[95] There were enough links between the two movements that, while "no regularly constituted State suffrage convention has ever been held…at the close of the annual Woman's Christian Temperance Union convention it is customary for the members of this body who favor the ballot for women to meet and elect the usual officers for [the votes for women branch] of the [WCTU's] work," recorded the official history of women's suffrage.

"For fifteen years before her death in 1899, Mrs. Clara A. McDiarmid was a leader, was president of the association and represented the State at the national conventions," the history continued.[96] The same Clara McDiarmid is reported as recording secretary of the WCTU in March 1888.[97] Later that year, she was treasurer.[98] She was involved with the WCTU, therefore, at the time when the headquarters opened in June. She attended the WCTU convention at Hope[99] and on June 2, 1888, it was reported in the same paper that Lydia M. Chace, Julia Clark, and Clara A. McDiarmid were signatories to a memorial to the State Democratic Convention—as representatives of "one thousand of [Arkansas's] best women"—urging civility in the coming convention and campaign.

The suffrage organization that McDiarmid headed as president from early 1888 was separate from the WCTU, but the members of the two organizations were often the same. Later both organizations used the offices that McDiarmid donated at 315 West Markham.

Today, the building at the former location of the headquarters of the WCTU is the Statehouse Convention Center, while the northern arm of the intersection of Main and Markham, which in 1888 led toward the river, is long gone.

In June 1888, the WCTU held "a reception at state headquarters, 106 E Markham Street" for anyone interested in temperance. The notice asked for donations to furnish the second-floor premises. In this image, of the Main and Markham intersection looking east, the WCTU was on the north side of Markham (left)—a building that the second, lower roofline possibly marks.
(Courtesy of the Butler Center for Arkansas Studies, Little Rock, Arkansas)

Chapter 12:
Votes for Women at the Board of Trade, Second and Scott Streets

Early in 1911, women in Little Rock set up the Political Equality League to work for women's suffrage. Initially, its "semi-monthly meetings were...held in the public library," but by October 1913, according to the official history of women's suffrage in the United States, the women met upstairs in the "Chamber of Commerce." There was no "Chamber of Commerce" in Little Rock at that time—it was the Board of Trade at Scott and Second Streets. It is unknown how long the Political Equality League held its meetings in the quaint 1887 Queen Anne–style[100] Board of Trade offices because the meetings were again moved elsewhere. "[F]ew people would climb two flights of stairs to hear a subject discussed in which there was little interest, so the executive board secured the parlors of the City Hall," the history records.[101]

The old Board of Trade on the southeast corner of Second and Scott is now the location of the Historic Arkansas Museum.

After Little Rock women founded their Political Equality League early in 1911, it scheduled frequent public meetings. By October 1913, they convened upstairs in the "Chamber of Commerce," which was actually the Board of Trade at Scott and Second. The stairs, however, proved to be an obstacle to potential participants, so the group moved from there to City Hall. (Courtesy of the Butler Center for Arkansas Studies, Little Rock, Arkansas)

Today, the site of what was once the Board of Trade at Second and Scott is the location of the Historic Arkansas Museum. (Photo by Ron Davis, 2010)

Chapter 13:
Kempner Theatre—
Carrie Chapman Catt Speaks in 1916,
500 Block, South Louisiana Street (1916)

In April 1916, suffragists took over the Kempner Theatre for a public lecture by nationally known suffragist Carrie Chapman Catt. Wisconsin-born Catt had risen through the Iowa suffrage movement from the late 1880s to the early 1890s, becoming involved in the National American Woman Suffrage Association (NAWSA) on the encouragement of Susan B. Anthony. She took the reins of the NAWSA from Anthony in 1900. After resigning from the presidency of the NAWSA in 1904 due to her husband's illness, Catt had become president of the NAWSA again in late 1915, replacing Rev. Anna Howard Shaw.

Catt assumed the leadership of the NAWSA at a crucial juncture in suffrage history. The NAWSA's long-term policy of campaigning for votes for women state by state seemed almost dead in the water with the defeat of suffrage amendments in November 1915 in New York, New Jersey, Pennsylvania, and Massachusetts.

Meanwhile, a new organization, which had actually arisen out of the NAWSA's Congressional Committee, was making huge strides in raising awareness and working to gather support for the federal amendment to the U.S. Constitution that Susan B. Anthony had lobbied to have introduced in the Congress in 1878. Since that time, the proposed amendment had come up for vote only once, in 1914—a premature vote that the NAWSA had engineered when not enough votes existed for victory and when the NAWSA strenuously opposed both the federal amendment approach and its proponents, such as Alice Paul and what was then the Congressional Union (later the National Woman's Party).

By the end of 1915, the vigorous work of Paul and her colleagues had made the policies of the NAWSA increasingly outmoded. This had played a part in Catt's reelection to the NAWSA presidency. In 1916, Catt began lobbying for the two major political parties to adopt a "votes for women" plank in their platforms, but they found that the parties would support women's suffrage only through state amendments. Catt faced playing serious catch-up if the NAWSA was to remain relevant; her visit to Little Rock took place just three months after Alice Paul had promoted the Congressional Union in the state. In the circumstances, Catt and her colleagues attracted quite a crowd.

One newspaper headline read: "Mrs. Carrie Chapman Catt, National Association President, and Mrs. Minnie Trumbull of Oregon Address Largely Attended Meeting at Kempner Theater." It stated, "Suffrage conditions in the United States, the chief opponents of woman suffrage and the remedies for this opposition, were discussed by Mrs. Carrie Chapman Catt, president of the National Woman Suffrage Association in a lecture at the Kempner Theater last night."[102]

Catt outlined the different groups that made up the opposition to women's suffrage, as she saw it—conservatives who did not care for any change; pessimists who believed that even men's suffrage had failed and that there was no reason to extend it to anyone else; and the "spoilers" who were unknowns with deep pockets who opposed women's suffrage purely because they could not use it to their own benefit.

Mrs. Minnie Trumbull began by addressing the audience as "Fellow citizens," adding, "Do you men not understand me? I said 'fellow citizens.' I shall vote for president in November."

As Oregon women had won the vote in 1912 when suffragists had forced a vote on women's suffrage by use of Oregon's ballot initiative, Trumbull's statement not only highlighted the fact that women already had the vote in some states, but it showed the inequalities across the country in voting rights. Without the vote, in her perspective, an individual was less than a citizen.

The Kempner Theatre was located at 512 South Louisiana Street.[103] Today, a parking lot associated with the former Lafayette Hotel occupies that approximate location.

Carrie Chapman Catt, president of the National American Woman Suffrage Association—the nation's largest suffrage group—spoke to a large crowd in the Kempner Theatre in April 1916, appearing along with local leaders Mrs. T. T. Cotnam and Mrs. O. F. Ellington. Also speaking was Minnie Trumbull of Oregon, where women had had equal suffrage since 1912. (Courtesy of Ray Hanley)

Listed at the 500 block of South Louisiana St. in the 1917 Polk City Directory, the Kempner Theatre's former location is now a private parking lot. (Photo by Ron Davis, 2011)

Chapter 14:
Carnegie Library, Seventh and
South Louisiana Streets (1911–1963)

In February 1911, a group of seventy-five people in Little Rock, mostly women, banded together to work for votes for women. They named the new organization the Political Equality League. It came into existence following the introduction in the Arkansas legislature of a bill to give women the vote—a move that ultimately failed. The Political Equality League, however, remained.

The *Gazette*, in its report on the new Political Equality League, noted, "The ultimate aim of the League is to secure equal suffrage but the members will be expected to take an interest in questions of legislative, municipal and home affairs."[104]

The league was divided into twelve departments, each with "a chairman [who] will be responsible for the program and efficiency of the work in her department." The educational department was to focus on teaching women about the league and about the issues the league was involved with. "The semi-monthly meetings were first held in the public library, one in the afternoon, the other at night, so that working women, teachers and men might attend," recorded the *History of Woman Suffrage* more than ten years later.[105]

The library, on Louisiana at Seventh, was known as the Carnegie Library. Opened in 1910, the then brand-new library continued as a meeting place for women campaigning for equal rights at the ballot box on and off for quite some time. In March 1917, when women anticipated victory in winning an act to give them the vote in primaries, many met at the library to learn about the vote and the campaigns women had fought to bring Arkansans to this point.

More than 200 women enrolled at the opening yesterday of the suffrage school at the Little Rock Public Library [held] under the auspices of the National [American] Woman Suffrage Association with the co-operation of the Arkansas Suffragist Association and the Little Rock Political Equality League.

The school was organized by Miss Ann Doughty of New York. Mrs. Halsay W. Wilson of White Plains, N.J. discussed "Suffrage History," reviewing the growth of the movement and the work of its great leaders.[106]

Wilson highly commended the work of Mrs. T. T. Cotnam of Little Rock in the recent work in New York. "We had no more valued worker than Mrs. Cotnam," she said. "She has rendered great service in the training of workers and extending the cause by publicity work. Cotnam, president of the main Arkansas suffrage league, had campaigned in New York in favor of the failed suffrage amendment there in 1915. She gave two talks during the [Suffrage School] day, discussing press work in the morning and public speaking in the afternoon. Doughty spoke in the afternoon on fundraising methods for suffrage work."[107]

The old Carnegie Library was demolished in 1963. The new building that replaced it is still in the same location, but the Main Library of the Central Arkansas Library System is now located on Rock Street, right downtown in the River Market district.

Little Rock's Carnegie Library opened its doors in 1910. The Women's Political Equality League started holding meetings there twice a month in early 1911. The library also hosted a Suffrage School in March 1917 during the two days before Governor Charles Hillman Brough signed into law the right of Arkansas women to vote in primaries. (Courtesy of the Butler Center for Arkansas Studies, Little Rock, Arkansas)

The old Carnegie Library was demolished in 1963 to make way for this more modern building, which became a data center for Entergy after the Central Arkansas Library System's Main Library moved to 100 Rock Street. The entrance columns of the Carnegie Library now stand opposite the entrance to today's Main Library. (Photo by Ron Davis, 2010)

Chapter 15:
The National Woman's Party at Royal Arcanum Hall, 105 West Eighth Street

When Mabel Vernon of the National Woman's Party (NWP) visited Little Rock in November 1917, newspapers announced that she was "scheduled for one regular speech, which is to be given at the city hall at 7 o'clock Tuesday night."[108] The *Gazette* had reported the talk would be in City Hall at 3 p.m. The Wednesday *Gazette*, however, reported that "approximately 45 women and five men were present at the meeting at the Royal Arcanum Hall yesterday afternoon. At the suggestion of Miss Vernon, a resolution was adopted to be sent to the president and members of Congress from Arkansas urging passing of a national suffrage amendment at the next session of Congress. Mrs. W. T. Roberts made the motion for the adoption of the resolution and Mrs. Mamie Lou Tabor seconded it."[109]

As no report appeared of Vernon's announced speech at City Hall, what actually happened would have remained a mystery if it were not for national sources for this local event in the suffrage campaign. While relating the history of the November 1917 tour by members of the NWP across the country to explain their picketing and hunger strikes, a national history states:

> Suddenly, while everything was apparently going smoothly, audiences large, indignantly sympathetic, actively protective, change came. Everywhere obstacles were put in the way of the speakers. That this was the result of concerted action on the part of the authorities was evident from the fact that within a few days four speakers in different parts of the country felt this blocking influence. In Arkansas they recalled Mabel Vernon's permit for the Court House (*sic*)...[110]

The hall where it is reported that Vernon spoke belonged to the Royal Arcanum Society, one of the many fraternal organizations of Little Rock at the time. "The Royal Arcanum...is a fraternal benefit life insurance company founded in Massachusetts in 1877, and which still boasted 28,111 members in 1994," reports one source, which also reveals the 1909 initiation ritual for members.[111] One Little Rock newspaper described its location in 1916 as the southwest corner of Eighth and Main.[112] The City Directory of 1917 listed it at 105 W Eighth Street, which more or less abutted the Majestic Theater at 806 Main.[113] Today, like so many of the suffrage sites of Little Rock, the location is a parking lot. No photo has yet emerged of what the building looked like.

National campaigner and picket prisoner Mabel Vernon of the NWP not only held a street meeting in Little Rock like the one shown here, but she also organized a rally in the Royal Arcanum Hall. Permission for her rally in City Hall had been revoked because local NAWSA suffragists disapproved of the methods, such as picketing the president and hunger strikes, that the NWP used to keep suffrage on the public agenda. The meeting at the Royal Arcanum Hall was held to explain Alice Paul's hunger strike and to protest her force-feeding by the Wilson administration. The rally sent a telegram to the president protesting the treatment of Paul and demanding suffrage for women. (Courtesy of the Records of the National Woman's Party, Library of Congress, Manuscript Division)

Chapter 16:
Mary W. Loughborough and the **Arkansas Ladies' Journal**, 723 South Main Street

In 1884, Mary W. Loughborough, who lived with her daughter at 901 Main Street in Little Rock,[114] began to publish a journal for women. Mary was the widow of James Loughborough, the land commissioner of the Cairo and Fulton (later Union Pacific) Railway. The town of Hope was named for their daughter. Mary Loughborough was known for her book, *My Cave Life in Vicksburg*, her memoir of the famous Civil War siege.

The publication began life as the *Ladies' Little Rock Journal* within the *Rural and Workman* newspaper on June 21, 1881. It later became the standalone *Arkansas Ladies' Journal* and finally the *Southern Ladies' Journal*.[115] The *Journal* was a huge new departure in the South, reported the *Woman's Journal of Boston and Chicago*—the long-established publication of the American women's suffrage movement, for it not only featured women's concerns, but it also took a stand on women's issues such as the vote.[116]

In 1886, the publication became the *Southern Ladies' Journal*. "[It] is a new candidate for public favor, and is the outgrowth from the *Arkansas Ladies' Journal*. It is well printed and skillfully edited, and has a long lease on life, many friends wish," reported the *Arkansas Gazette*.[117]

The *Southern Ladies' Journal* "is issued by a stock company of ladies of which Mrs. M. W. Loughborough is president. It has the benefit of the large circulation of the paper of which this is the growth," also reported the *Arkansas Gazette*[118] "and is altogether a bright and interesting journal." The journal had its own presses, reported the *Woman's Journal of Boston*.[119]

For some time, at least during its first year, the journal had business offices on Main Street. An item in the first edition—June 21, 1884—noted, "All communications or subscriptions intended for *Little Rock Ladies' Journal* will please be directed to, or handed in their office at Wilson & Webb's Bookstore."[120] According to the 1884 Sholes City Directory, this was 212 Main, but elsewhere it is listed as 210 Main.[121]

The "uptown" editorial offices started at 9th and Main[122] while a business office—for placing adverts and other notices—remained at Wilson & Webb's. However, in late 1886, consolidation took place, which gives valuable insight not only into women's reform work, but also into a business run by woman: "New and complete quarters, upon the ground floor, corner of Eighth and Main Streets will contain printing office, press and mechanical department for The Journal work, and for job printing. While the front room, with glass doors opening on Main Street, will be used as our business office and as a reception room for our many kind friends, whom we hope will call at any time as we can assure them a cordial welcome."[123]

In 1887, the Southern Ladies' Journal Printing Co. is listed at 723 Main Street—also the residence of Loughborough's daughter, Miss Jean W. Loughborough.[124] This may be an indication that Jean, who also wrote for the *Journal*, like many female entrepreneurs even today, produced this pioneering publication out of her home. It could be said that she "lived above the store." That same directory lists the *Southern Ladies' Journal*'s location as "the [northeast] corner Main and 8th, Mrs. M. W. Loughborough, Editor."[125]

On February 16, 1887, the *Arkansas Gazette* reported: "The *Southern Ladies' Journal*, conducted by Mrs. Mary W. Loughborough, will be enlarged by additional pages and hereafter issued semi-monthly instead of weekly. It is a most deserving publication which deserves a generous support."

These February plans never worked out, in a failure that demonstrates the fragility of life and the equal fragility of women's work for reform in that era—that month, Loughborough took seriously ill and died unexpectedly on August 27. The *Gazette* reported on the sorrow of her friends at the passing of a much respected and talented woman.[126]

The *Journal*[127] died with her, reported another new women's venture, the *Woman's Chronicle*, on March 3, 1888.[128]

The parking lot adjacent to the Donaghey Building in the 700 block of Main Street, which bridges to the 800 block, now occupies the site where Loughborough conducted her pioneering venture for women at 723 Main Street. Mary W. Loughborough is buried in Mount Holly Cemetery in Little Rock.

The first business office of the Arkansas Ladies' Journal *was in Wilson & Webb's Bookstore, listed at 210 Main Street in the 1880s. On the west side of Main, it would have occupied what was by the late 1950s/early 1960s the Hardy's shoestore location.* (Courtesy of the Arkansas History Commission, Little Rock, Arkansas)

This huge modern parking lot at Eighth and Main covers the location of the offices of the Arkansas' Ladies Journal *described by the editors in 1886.* (Photo by Ron Davis, 2011)

The distinctive masthead of the Arkansas Ladies' Journal *of the 1880s. The* Arkansas Ladies' Journal—*originally the* Little Rock Ladies' Journal *and later the* Southern Ladies' Journal—*first appeared in 1884 and broke new ground in the South. It died with its publisher, Mary Loughborough, in 1887.* (Courtesy of the Arkansas History Commission, Little Rock, Arkansas)

Jean Loughborough Douglass worked with her mother on the Arkansas Ladies' Journal *in the 1880s. (Courtesy of Mary Mark Ockerbloom, editor,* A Celebration of Women Writers)

Ellen Maria Harrell Cantrell, born in Virginia and living at 619 Scott Street, Little Rock, in the 1890s, wrote fiction for magazines, newspaper articles, and editorials, and served as associate editor of the Arkansas Ladies' Journal. *(Courtesy of Mary Mark Ockerbloom, editor,* A Celebration of Women Writers)

Chapter 17:
YMCA—Carrie Chapman Catt in 1900, 717–719 South Main Street (1900)

When Carrie Chapman Catt visited Little Rock in April 1900, she spoke at the YMCA hall "to a fair sized and appreciative audience."[129] Catt's lineage in suffrage was impressive: Susan B. Anthony, the nation's leading nineteenth-century women's rights campaigner, had chosen Catt to succeed her in the National American Woman Suffrage Association (NAWSA), and Catt became president when her mentor retired in 1900. Catt's visit to Little Rock that May was part of a suffrage tour of the South. Her talk was free to the public.

The YMCA hall was at "Eighth and Main streets," the *Arkansas Democrat* reported.[130] The city directory at the time listed the address as 717–719 South Main—still the same location shown on the Sanborn map of 1897.[131]

Catt's lecture was a great success. Although scheduled to leave on April 26 for New Orleans, according to the *Gazette*, an originally un-scheduled lecture was planned for the evening following her YMCA talk. The *Democrat* reported: "No admission will be charged and the public is cordially invited, being assured that they will spend a most delightful evening."[132]

The day before, the same paper had already said this of Catt:

> She is spoken of as a word artist of rare ability. Her lectures are notable for their excellence both in diction and delivery. Her sentences are word pictures and the elevated sentiments conveyed give a practical value to the truths she conveys. She is a woman of fine presence and broad culture. Her public life as a lecturer in a cause which even yet meets with so much opposition has not left its mark of defiant

boldness upon her as it so often does upon women reformers and lec-
turers. She is a personally magnetic woman who never antagonizes
her hearers but by persuasive argument and clear reasoning appeals
to their brains and their hearts and their sense of justice.[133]

The similarity between this *Democrat* report and that of the *Gazette*
the next day indicates that some good public relations material may
have been delivered to them in advance of Catt's visit. Unfortunately,
the newspapers did not report what she actually said.

Carrie Chapman Catt,
who was president of
the National American
Woman Suffrage
Association when
women won the right to
vote with the 19th
Amendment.
(Courtesy of the
Library of Congress,
National Photo
Company Collection)

Chapter 18:
Suffrage Organization 1.0—An 1888 Arkansas Mystery, Turner Studio, 814 Main Street

Around the time that Arkansas women won the vote through the 19th Amendment to the U.S. Constitution, there was obviously some debate about the history of the women's suffrage movement in Little Rock of thirty years before—specifically, questions of where the Arkansas Equal Suffrage Association of the late nineteenth century was founded. This debate is clear in an article of February 1919, in which the author discusses Susan B. Anthony's visit to Little Rock in "July 1889": "While interest was fresh and alive from her visit, a league was organized in Little Rock, with Mrs. Clara McDiarmid president. The first meeting of the league was held in Mrs. Turner's studio, in which was then called the Allis block. The late Mrs. Myra MacAlmont Vaughan had in her possession one of the postals upon which the invitations to the meeting were written."[134]

Mrs. S. S. Wassell was a suffragist at the time of this *Arkansas Gazette* article—Congress had not yet passed the 19th Amendment proposal, so ratification by any state was still several months away. She was described in her byline as "Chairman, History Committee," but her organization is not given. It is likely she belonged to the Arkansas Equal Suffrage State Central Committee, the successor to the state suffrage organization that had been formed in Little Rock in October 1914.

Wassell made some mistakes in her article, for Anthony's visit was actually in February 1889, while the Arkansas Equal Suffrage Association was established in February 1888. In fact, it is very likely that Anthony's visit came about because of the Little Rock association.

However, Wassell is correct that the Arkansas Equal Suffrage Association was founded in Turner's studio. Clara McDiarmid recorded it in a letter to the Boston-based *Woman's Journal* soon after the organization's founding:

> The first move toward an equal suffrage association has been made, and an Arkansas Equal Suffrage Association was organized last Friday, at the studio of Mrs. Carrie Turner. Mrs. Jenkins (teacher) was elected vice-president; Prof. Ida Brooks corresponding secretary; Miss Brown (editor Sunday Life) recording secretary; Mrs. Wallace (teacher) treasurer; Mrs. Hart (State organizer W.C.T.U.) vice-president-at large; Mrs. Chunn, of Clarksville, also vice-president-at-large.
>
> We are distributing leaflets, have a committee on programmes, and are to have two papers at each monthly meeting. Innumerable obstacles to overcome, but "onward" is the watchword.[135]

McDiarmid signed the letter, "Pres. E.S.A." on February 25, 1888.

But where was Turner's studio? According to the extant city directory closest to the time, Turner's studio opened on October 9, 1885, at 814 Main Street.[136] She was listed there in the 1886 city directory. Assuming Turner had not moved by 1888, it was here that the Arkansas Equal Suffrage Association was founded that February. However, there is some doubt about this, for in 1887, Turner's residence was listed at 417 Rock Street in the city directory,[137] but there is no studio listing. There is no reference to her in later directories. Turner's studio may very well have been in the Allis Block on Markham Street opposite the Old State House—right beside where Clara McDiarmid put up a building and donated space for women's groups to meet in 1889. McDiarmid's only contemporary source and Wassell's story thirty years later, therefore, together create an Arkansas suffrage mystery. While Myra MacAlmont Vaughan's "postal," to which Wassell referred, may have proven the truth of the matter, it has not yet surfaced.

Chapter 19:
The Radical Suffragists and Adolphine Fletcher Terry's Home, 411 East Seventh Street

What is known today as the Arkansas Arts Center Community Gallery in Little Rock at 411 East Seventh Street was the lifelong home of Adolphine Fletcher Terry, famed as the leader of the women of the Women's Emergency Committee to Open Our Schools, which fought to reopen Little Rock's schools during the desegregation crisis of the 1950s. But the historic link of the home to civil rights goes far back before that time—to the first decades of the twentieth century and the struggle for the right of women to vote.[138]

Terry's sister, Mary Fletcher, who owned the home with Terry, was the first president of the Woman's Political Equality League (WPEL), founded in February 1911 at the same time as an unsuccessful measure was before the General Assembly to give Arkansas women the vote. Mary Fletcher was president of the WPEL for only a short time, but she worked again for women's rights when a state suffrage organization was being created in October 1914.[139]

Terry's early involvement in suffrage is recorded in local lore,[140] and the official history of women's suffrage, published in 1922, also reports on Terry's role in the campaign.[141] These reports indicate some involvement of Terry in suffrage, but they supply little detail. Further information emerges elsewhere, however, shining a completely different light on her suffrage work.

The local lore and official history only report Terry working in support of the largest suffrage organization, the National American Woman Suffrage Association (NAWSA), confirmed when she delivered a short speech at the luncheon held at the Marion Hotel during the visit of Carrie Chapman Catt, president of the NAWSA, in the spring of 1916.[142] But Terry also took a very public stand for suffrage in support of the Congressional Union, later the National Woman's Party (NWP)—the organization that finally forged the success of the forty-two-year-old campaign for a constitutional amendment to guarantee women's right to vote. Susan B. Anthony had launched what became the 19th Amendment to the U.S. Constitution in 1878—thirty years after women first called for the right to vote at Seneca Falls, New York, in 1848. The overall campaign took seventy-two years.

In January 1916, Terry very publicly presided at a conference at the Marion Hotel when Alice Paul and Mabel Vernon of what was then the Congressional Union arrived in Little Rock to create a local branch and raise funds. While the NAWSA members attended this meeting, they held their distance, saying that any funds they gathered went to the NAWSA.[143]

In November 1917, Mabel Vernon revisited the local branch of the Congressional Union, now named the National Woman's Party, during a tour to explain the reasons for the NWP's picketing of the White House and to relate details of the picketers' imprisonments—the hunger strikes for political status that Alice Paul and others were on and the force-feeding that the Wilson administration was subjecting them to. During this trip, which the local affiliate of the NAWSA strongly objected to, the advance guard of Mabel Vernon made arrangements for a "home visit"[144] with local members of the NWP, including Terry.[145] Terry remained behind the scenes on this occasion, and it might reasonably be claimed she was distancing herself from the NWP because of their so-called "militancy," which set the women up against the commander in chief.

Yet Terry's name remained in the NWP's National Advisory Committee in its national publication, the *Suffragist*, until after ratification in 1920. A more likely reason for Terry's reticence at this time, apart from being busy with personal matters, was the anti-German sentiment, very strong in Little Rock, which erupted when the United States declared war on Germany. Terry's family was of German origin, and she mentioned the anti-German sentiment later in life.[146]

Whether any NWP members ever visited Terry at home, her home will always be connected with civil rights—not only civil rights of African Americans but also the civil rights of women—because of Terry's support of the group that won for American women the right to vote, and for the work of her sister, Mary Fletcher.

The Fletcher sisters—two of Arkansas's suffragists—grew up in this house in the 400 block of 7th Street. Mary was the first president of the Woman's Political Equality League founded in 1911. Adolphine, as Mrs. D. D. Terry, chaired Alice Paul's meeting in Little Rock in 1916 and became a member of the NWP's National Advisory Committee, remaining in that position until 1920.
(Courtesy of the Butler Center for Arkansas Studies, Little Rock, Arkansas)

Adolphine Fletcher Terry gave this photo to the National Woman's Party in 1916 when she became a member of its National Advisory Committee. It appeared in the Suffragist *newspaper in February 1916. (Courtesy of the Library of Congress, Manuscript Division)*

Chapter 20:
Where Women Marched—
Parades, Meetings, and Other Activities

ittle Rock's streets—not only its buildings—served as a stage for the city's suffragists in their drawn-out campaign for votes for women. The parades began early in the suffrage era, indicating how strongly women felt about having the right to vote, for marching in public was not considered "womanly." The first suffrage parade took place in the 1890s. Mrs. S. S. Wassell, in an article published in 1919, wrote: "About 1890 Mrs. Lida Merriweather of Tennessee was advertized to give 12 lectures under the auspices of the National Suffrage Society of Arkansas. Just before the lecture in Little Rock, the league, then consisting of some half dozen members, marched down Markham and Main street carrying a banner announcing the time and place of the lecture. So there was a real suffrage parade in Little Rock nearly 30 years ago."[147]

That is the only suffrage march on record from around that time, and the story comes from a report many years later, so its accuracy is not certain. In fact, the date may be out by more than half a decade, for the *History of Woman Suffrage* recorded that Mrs. Merriweather's lecture visit took place in 1896. Either way, the suffrage march could have been the first-ever such march in the United States.[148]

A march definitely was held on Suffrage Day in 1914. On May 2, suffragists persuaded business owners on Main Street to decorate their stores in honor of the event,[149] and a procession went from the rally at the Old State House to the celebratory luncheon at the Capital Hotel. In 1916, during the visit of the president of the National American Woman Suffrage Association (NAWSA), it was reported that "Mrs.

[Carrie Chapman] Catt, accompanied by Mrs. Minnie Trumbull, suffrage worker of Oregon, and Mrs. T. T. Cotnam of Little Rock Political Equality League, arrived in Little Rock yesterday afternoon. They were met at the Rock Island station by a large number of suffrage supporters. Eighteen automobiles, decorated with suffrage emblems, paraded the streets for a half hour after the distinguished workers' arrival. Many out-of-town suffragists came to hear the addresses."[150]

In 1916, Little Rock suffragists were out in front during the Pulaski County fair parade, winning first prize:

[Despite rain, the automobiles] that were dressed for...the decorated automobile parade feature of the second day of the Pulaski County Fair...drew crowds that lined both sides of Main street for a number of blocks...

A party of suffragists in a new Studebaker machine decorated in yellow and white, the colors of the "Votes for Women" cause, easily was the prettiest car of the parade, and judges did not hesitate in making the first award to them.

The entry was by the Little Rock Political Equality League, an organization of 300 women of the city. The work was designed and done by a committee of which Miss Norma Hutton was chairman. The body of the car was in yellow cotton blossoms with fenders and trimmings in white, showing the different stages of development of the flower. Over the hood was a large hand-painted butterfly. More than 4,000 separate pieces were used in the decoration. The occupants included Miss Hutton, Miss Emil Knox, Mrs. Chauncey Warren, Mrs. Drennan Scott and Mrs. Frank W. Gibb. The prize awarded is $50 cash, offered by the Little Rock Motor Club...

The pageant started at Markham and Gaines streets, moved to Fourteenth and Main and back to Capitol Avenue, thence east two blocks, where it disbanded. Judges were stationed at Capitol avenue and Main street while the parade was moving south, and then took a post on east Capitol avenue to make a second review.[151]

In 1917, the NAWSA organized a Suffrage School at the Carnegie Library that coincided with the passage of the bill whereby women won the vote in primary elections. A meeting at the Marion Hotel was preceded by a parade of cars: "Before the mass meeting [at the Marion Hotel] an automobile parade and demonstration was held downtown. Led by a drum corps, the long line of gaily decorated automobiles filled with elated suffrage workers left Capitol Avenue and Main Street at 7:15."[152]

There is no report of controversy at the time of any of these events, but controversy swirled around the National Woman's Party (NWP) when its members came to Little Rock in November 1917 to explain why they were picketing the White House.[153] On November 10, 1917, Jane Pincus of New York and Dorothy Craycroft of Oklahoma—"advance agents" of NWP leader Mabel Vernon—held "an open air meeting from an automobile at Fourth and Main streets." The car "was decorated in the suffrage colors of purple, white and gold" and the crowd that heard Pincus talk "was not a large" one.[154] Pincus and Craycroft found when they arrived in Little Rock that the members of the local affiliate of the major suffragist group were annoyed:

> "The National Woman's Party is for national woman's suffrage," Miss Pincus began, as she stood on the rear seat of an automobile. "Women are the only class of disfranchised people in this country. The laborers have the Democratic party and the negroes the Republican party, but the women have no voice in the affairs of the nation. They must wait patiently as they have done for 70 years. The suffrage amendment has been before Congress for 49 years, as we are still waiting...
>
> The only effective and dignified way of getting suffrage is to turn all of our attention to Washington, to keep the matter before the officials at all times...
>
> It would require only one hour's time to pass this amendment to the constitution..."[155]

Just over a week later, Mabel Vernon "who has been arrested and sent to jail three times for picketing in front of the White House,"[156] reported the *Arkansas Gazette*, addressed a crowd at the same venue— the same intersection where, more than forty years later, black students from Philander Smith College started a lunch-counter sit-in at Woolworth's to protest race discrimination. In 1917, Vernon spoke passionately of what happened in Washington when women campaigned for the right to vote:

> One of our banners said, "How long, Mr. President, must the women of this country wait for liberty?" You men may not realise [sic] that

we have worked 70 years for suffrage in this country. We women have been more patient than men in our fight for liberty. Men have never hesitated to burn, to murder, even to die for political rights. We have only sought by peaceful means to secure a voice in this government. We hope that no one even will need to die in the cause of suffrage. They will not dare keep Alice Paul in prison until it kills her. To retreat now in the face of persecution would be to acknowledge ourselves to be in the wrong. We must go on.[157]

Alice Paul, the leader and chief strategist of the NWP (which conducted the picketing), was being force-fed in jail in Washington DC when on a hunger strike for political prisoner status. Interestingly, under a headline, "Chilly Reception, Just as Forecast—Picket-Orators Arouse Little Enthusiasm in Small Audiences," the *Arkansas Gazette* reported that, after Vernon and her assistant Natalie Gray of Colorado Springs "with the assistance of two men pushed a big car out of the location she wanted for her car...A crowd of 150 people soon gathered" at Fourth and Main where the suffragists spoke. Such a crowd is not small.

While the news story reported some opposition to the NWP cause, its headline seemed to reflect local opinion rather than fact—the local opinion in this case being the displeasure of the local affiliate members of the NAWSA when they publicly promised the NWP representatives "a Jack Frost welcome." Vernon and Gray "talked nearly two hours and a half," the *Gazette* reported—and it said that "the crowd became rather thin toward the end," which, presumably, was understandable, as the talk was long and "the night was chilly."

Suffragists had infiltrated countless activities in Little Rock. July 24, 1919, saw the third annual Suffrage Ball Day[158] at Kavanaugh Field, when the local suffrage organization received part of game receipts. Kavanaugh Park was on Park Avenue between 14th and 16th Streets.[159] A report about the day read: "Arrangements yesterday were made for Suffrage Day Thursday [July 24, 1919] at Kavanaugh Field by the Pulaski County Suffrage Association, when the Travelers and Barons play. One day is set aside each baseball season as Suffrage Day, on which the suffrage organization receives a percentage of the proceeds as well as being permitted to sell refreshments at the game."[160]

Just a few days later, at the special session called to ratify the 19th Amendment, yet another parade of women gathered, this time descending on the State Capitol, where repeatedly during this suffrage decade women had converged demanding votes for women. The *Arkansas Gazette* reported a statement from the women: "We feel absolutely certain that the Arkansas legislature in special session tomorrow will ratify the Susan B. Anthony amendment....A large delegation of women from over the state are expected. We will be at the state capitol at 11:30 a.m. to receive informally the legislators and show them our appreciation of their services."[161]

The busy Fourth and Main intersection was where members of the National Woman's Party held several street meetings in November 1917 during Mabel Vernon's cross-country trip to rally support for Alice Paul, who was being force-fed in prison while on a hunger strike. (Courtesy of Ray Hanley)

Little Rock's Rock Island Station, ca. 1910, just six years before Little Rock suffragists converged on the station to welcome national campaigners arriving there and to begin a suffrage parade through the city's streets. Today the building is part of the Clinton School of Public Service. (Source: Author's Collection)

On March 31, 1916, local NAWSA leaders Mrs. T. T. Cotnam and Mrs. O. F. Ellington arrived at Rock Island Station with national suffrage leaders Carrie Chapman Catt and Minnie Trumbull for rallies in Little Rock. These women and a procession of decorated autos led a suffrage procession through Little Rock's streets after their arrival. (Source: *Arkansas Gazette*, April 1, 1916.)

Local and National Leaders of the Cause in Big Rally Here

This photograph was taken at the Rock Island station yesterday afternoon immediately after the arrival of the distinguished visitors. From left to right—Mrs. Carrie Chapman Catt, Mrs. T. T. Cotnam, Mrs. Minnie Trumbull and Mrs. O. F. Ellington.

Jane Pincus of the National Woman's Party came to Little Rock in November 1917 to help organize rallies in support of imprisoned suffragist Alice Paul. The news story of her arrival in Little Rock said her street meetings would display some of the banners that had "started the trouble" in Washington. Yet all the picketing was peaceful; attacking crowds had "started the trouble," and the Wilson administration had imprisoned the women illegally. (Source: Arkansas Gazette, November 10, 1917, 1.)

Chapter 21:
The McDiarmid House, 1424 Center Street

The McDiarmid House at 1424 Center Street is one of the most important early sites of women's suffrage activity in Little Rock. Clara McDiarmid lived there during her most active time in the struggle for women's suffrage between about 1888 and 1895. McDiarmid was the most prominent of the leaders of the suffrage movement in the city in the late nineteenth century, representing Little Rock at the state level and Arkansas both at the regional and national level. She also represented the state for the Woman's Christian Temperance Union in London in 1895. That year is the approximate end of the clear association of the McDiarmid House with the struggle for women's rights in Little Rock.

McDiarmid lived in the house in February 1888 when the Arkansas Equal Suffrage Association (AESA) was formed. It is likely that she was at home when she wrote the letter to the *Woman's Journal* of Boston about that event, which took place "at the studio of Mrs. Carrie Turner." The founding of the AESA occurred around February 25, 1888—the date McDiarmid signed her letter, "Pres. E.S.A."[162]

Clara Alma Cox McDiarmid was born in Noblesville, Indiana, in 1847.[163] Her grandmother was Lydia Sexton, a renowned preacher who became the first female prison chaplain in Kansas. Sexton's first son, John Thomas Cox Jr., and his wife, Catherine Rowan Allison, were Clara's parents. Clara came to Little Rock during the summer of 1866 from Ottumwa, Kansas, where she had been a teacher.[164] That August, she married Captain George W. McDiarmid, then stationed at the Little Rock Arsenal. The next month, George was discharged. By March, 1868 he was in politics as Pulaski County Clerk.

In 1871, George McDiarmid inherited part ownership of the land that the house at 1424 Center Street sits on. His mother, Elizabeth Osborn, had bought that land and contiguous lots in 1867. Later, the joint ownership with his sister was ultimately wholly conveyed via George W. McDiarmid, to his and Clara's son, George C. McDiarmid, when the child was only about thirty months old. This occurred in 1873 and the house remained in the family for more than two decades.

Property and tax records show that Clara McDiarmid's home—the historic property today—was built between 1880 and 1883. Although unsettled street numbers make it difficult to pin down events exactly, it seems that the McDiarmids resided there starting in approximately 1883. At the least, street directories establish that Clara McDiarmid was very definitely associated with 1424 Center Street by 1887, and this association continues definitely until about 1895. During this era, 1424 Center Street was directly linked through McDiarmid with suffrage. For this reason, it merits recognition as one of the earliest civil rights sites in Little Rock.

In 1891, one of Clara McDiarmid's frequent soirées left a record of what 1424 Center Street looked like inside:

> The spacious parlors were handsomely decorated with palms, ferns and vines, which added much to the rare beauty of the furnishings. The house has recently been remodeled, and it is artistic and homelike in the extreme. The furnishing throughout has been done with an eye to color, and the delicate drapery and unique furniture of Nile green and gold blend harmoniously, and form a picture that lingers long in memory. The hostess looked regal in black velvet en train, and was assisted in receiving by Mesdames Ayres and Adams. Refreshments were served in an elegant manner, and the floral decorations of the table added much to the appetizing viands spread for the refreshing of the inner man.[165]

In July 1889, Clara McDiarmid hosted the Arkansas Equal Suffrage Association at home. This was billed as a "Sunflower Tea" and the report of the meeting demonstrates some of her style.

> Cards of invitation were decorated with yellow ribbon....On each... was written a quotation from some master brain, bearing on the subject, and as the roll was called each lady answered by reading her quotation.

Sunflowers were arranged in tasteful profusion about the apartments and lent an air of loyalty befitting the occasion. The refreshments were handsomely served. Cards of invitation also contained the menu, which was unique and most original.

Between thirty and forty ladies were present. The program consisted of music, readings and general discussion of topics of interest.[166]

The sunflower was the women's suffrage emblem, and yellow was the color of the cause. During the evening, Haryot Holt Cahoon delivered a paper about women's rights, sounding a ringing cry down the years from the parlor of 1424 Center Street from women who were betrayed in the Reconstruction Amendments and who, as they frequently pointed out, in spite of not having any representation, paid taxes and worked to improve society for all.[167] Women late in the nineteenth century were supposed to be passive, but this paper strongly protested this discrimination against woman. Among other things, Cahoon declared, "Woman is—and no doubt about it—the greatest discovery of the Nineteenth century. She was the one new thing under the sun."

Also in October 1891, another event at 1424 Center Street demonstrated the significance (and status) of Arkansas's organized suffrage women:

The beautiful home of Mrs. Clara McDiarmid was the scene of gayety and beauty…this week. The occasion was a reception given by Mrs. McDiarmid in honor of Dr. Ida [Joe] Brooks, who has recently returned to our city as a practicing physician. The reception was a regal affair, as are all entertainments given by this charming hostess. The ladies receiving were Mrs. McDiarmid, in pearl gray silk à la princesse with three-quarter sleeves trimmed with gray chiffons; Dr. Brooks, black silk, yellow chrysanthemums, yellow ribbon and chiffon; Mrs. Lura Brown, black silk, and jet ornaments; Mrs. Mary Burt Brooks, black lace and yellow dahlias; Dr. Cooper in a handsome black lace, V-neck and green chiffon trimming.

After a pleasant chat the guests passed to the supper room, where the menu was daintily served. At the plate of each guest was placed a dainty souvenir card with appropriate quotations.

Altogether a most delightful evening was enjoyed by all, and will long be remembered by the participants.[168]

The importance of this event is two-fold. Firstly, the fashions demonstrate clearly the social class of the suffragists. The event also reveals a gathering of the movers and shakers of the women's rights movement of Little Rock at the time. The hostess was the president of the Arkansas Woman Suffrage Association, the state organization affiliated to the National American Woman Suffrage Association, recently formed from the National Woman Suffrage Association and the American Woman Suffrage Association[169]; Dr. Ida Joe Brooks was a suffragist who had just broken through barriers in the medical profession; Miss Lura Brown, also a suffragist, was a journalist from Little Rock[170] and former assistant editor of *The Life, of Little Rock*; and Mrs. Mary Burt Brooks was an associate editor of the *Woman's Chronicle*. A journalist on duty likely could have reported on (but did not) some pointed opinions on suffrage, temperance, and other concerns of women, especially as Dr. Ida Joe Brooks, while studying in Boston, attended and reported on suffrage in Arkansas at the annual conventions of the Massachusetts Suffrage Association[171], and Clara McDiarmid had attended national conventions herself. The Arkansas Woman Suffrage Association, even if small, was a group with strong national links.

McDiarmid died on July 22, 1899, while in Des Moines, Iowa. She is buried in Oakland Fraternal Cemetery in Little Rock.

This house at 1424 Center saw many meetings of suffrage women. Its mistress, Clara A. McDiarmid, likely was here when she wrote the letter to the Woman's Journal *of Boston—a national newspaper—telling readers of the formation of the Arkansas Equal Suffrage Association in February 1888.* (Photograph by Bernadette Cahill, 2015)

Chapter 22:
Suffrage Organization 2.0—Lulu Markwell's Home, 1911, 1422 Rock Street

The meeting that formed the Women's Political Equality League (WPEL), as reported in the *Arkansas Gazette* in 1911, took place at 1422 Rock Street, the home of Lulu Markwell, who had been a member of the Woman's Christian Temperance Union (WCTU) for many years. The idea of the WPEL seems to have been born around January 20, 1911, when state representatives Grant of Jackson County and Whittington of Garland County "introduced a resolution [in the Arkansas legislature] providing that all women 21 years old and over be allowed the right of suffrage."[172]

"If every negro in the State is allowed to cast his vote on questions of State importance, even though he may not own a foot of land or possess enough property to be recorded on the assessor's books, then I see no reason why women should not be allowed to vote," said Whittington, in discussing the matter after the resolution had been introduced.[173]

This was a race-based argument which avoided bigger issues. If Whittington had said that women should be allowed to vote as citizens because *all* men had the right to vote and that to give them the vote would be a matter of justice, it could too easily have raised questions about the meaning of equality and how far such equality should go—into equal pay and opportunity and equality under the law for women with men, for example. If the notion that, purely for reasons of justice, women should vote equally with men *did* cross his mind, therefore, he did not say so.

Instead, he based his support of votes for women on expediency because it was more convenient politically. The argument that he used in 1911—black men's voting rights[174]—actually turned on its head the argument used fifty years before. At the time of the vicious enfranchisement controversies during Reconstruction, the fact that freedmen would be given the vote was employed repeatedly to exclude women—necessary, it was said, because enfranchising freedmen was reform enough for the nation to absorb at one time. A sound, practical reason for many, such arguments also enabled politicians to establish strict limits on voting reforms. The same kind of reasoning was also very convenient for politicians who balked at the idea of facing such a huge unknown as a female electorate. Yet what the politicians did on grounds of expediency—limit voting rights to only males—certainly gave no justice to the female half of the population that the 1860s sex qualification for the vote excluded.

Whittington's gesture of supporting votes for women may have made him appear in favor of suffrage for all, but that would have been true only if his argument had been based on the principle of equality of citizens, not on extending the vote to a group of people based on sex because a group of people of a specific race was already allowed to vote. Whittington's support of votes for women, although advanced for contemporary politicians and apparently magnanimous, masked the limited nature of his thinking and that of many others at the time.

Little Rock women were interested in this suffrage development, however, and when the resolution was before the Constitutional Committee, a "group of thirty-four…ranging in age from women of 70 to girls of 15 and including several well-known society leaders,"[175] having understood that they had a meeting with the committee, arrived at the State Capitol—only to find that the committee members had failed to show up.

The organization of the WPEL came about almost as a protest against this behavior. The "suffragettes" who attempted to deliver their mandate to the Constitutional Committee "went into the gallery and listened to the debate in the house, but after adjournment they met in the house chamber and organized."[176] This was the point at which the women decided to form an active suffrage movement.

As reported in the *Arkansas Gazette*, "The next meeting has been called for Saturday at the residence of Mrs. J. W. Markwell, 1422 Rock street, at which time the organization will be perfected…They declare that they are not militant suffragettes, but expect to organize and present their claims for the right to vote."[177]

The formal WPEL was the result, as reported in the *Gazette* on February 26, 1911: "The officers elected yesterday for the ensuing year were as follows: Miss Mary Fletcher, president; Mrs. W. P. Hutton, first vice-president; Miss Marguerite English, second vice-president; Mrs. Sutton, recording secretary; Miss Gatlin, corresponding secretary, and Miss Julia Warren, treasurer….Eight men have joined the league… [among them] Dr. J. W. Markwell and Clio Harper."

Members of this organization were active the next month when the suffrage bill was voted down.

The location of Lulu Markwell's house at 1422 Rock Street was an empty lot for some time, and there seems to be no photograph of her home there in 1911. Late in 2010, the construction of new homes began at Rock and Fifteenth where Little Rock's WPEL "was perfected" a hundred years before.

Lulu Markwell's home at 1422 Rock Street in 1911 occupied the corner of 15th and Rock, where the modern corner home sits today on the far left of this photo. Contemporary maps show the Markwell home in a building that faced both Rock and 15th streets. There is no 1422 Rock Street today. From late 2010, the southern half of the block has been filled in with single-family dwellings. (Photo by Bernadette Cahill, 2015)

Chapter 23:
The New State Capitol

Much suffrage activity took place at Arkansas's State Capitol from 1911 until the General Assembly met on July 28, 1919, and voted to ratify the 19th Amendment to the U.S. Constitution. This would finally guarantee women the vote after a campaign of more than seventy years. The women's suffrage campaign is considered the first successful non-violent civil rights campaign in U.S. history.

As reported in the *Arkansas Gazette*, the women's lobbying at the State Capitol began in 1911:

> Thirty-four strong, the suffragettes of Little Rock marched upon the Constitutional Committee of the House of Representatives of the Arkansas General Assembly yesterday afternoon, only to find that the members of this committee had "silently folded their tents and stolen away" with the exception of one lone Republican member, who stood before the advancing host and declared with fear and trembling that he knew nothing of the engagement the suffragettes declared that they had with the committee. Immediately after the house adjourned the suffragettes took possession of the House of Representatives and hoisted their banner in the campaign for "votes for women" in Arkansas.[178]

This happened on February 18, 1911, and it was the first time suffragists had lobbied for votes for women in the new State Capitol, as the state's General Assembly had begun to meet there only the previous January, having just moved from the Old State House. It must have been a thrilling sight, even if the House was emptying, when the women raised their banner; state representatives and officers of the assembly must have still been milling around. This reference to women hoisting a banner calling for votes for women in the State Capitol—whether literally or metaphorically—was only the start: women rallied there regularly as the campaign ratcheted up until its climax less than a decade later.

The February 1911 event arose in response to the bill that Representatives Grant of Jackson County and Whittington of Garland County had introduced to enfranchise women over 21 years of age. "Although the bill was greeted with applause, no discussion was made and it was referred to the Committee on Constitutional Amendments," the Gazette had reported on January 21.

Why the two members at that time had decided to introduce their bill is not clear. Their motivation may have been personal; perhaps they were urged by female family members, for the issue was not yet a hugely popular one. An editorial in the Arkansas Democrat said on February 15, 1911:

> It seems there will always be the agitation by some for the right of suffrage for women, but the great majority of the American women are content to be a potent influence in managing the affairs of the country, and care nothing for the right to cast a ballot.
>
> Few of them in this country would vote if they had the right...
>
> It is the woman without home life, more often, who must needs have something to employ her mind, and, having tired of theater parties, card parties and poodles, her mind naturally reverts to the suffrage question.[179]

This editorial went on to say that mothers raising their children well is a more important influence in politics than women campaigning for the vote—a reiteration of the century-old "Republican Motherhood" justification for keeping women out of politics. It claimed:

> It is not likely that woman suffrage will come in this country soon; surely not in the next generation or the next, and it is not likely that it will be the boon some women think it will be when it comes, if it ever does.
>
> The women of the country are protected by every law on the statute books....The woman is safer now without the ballot than she ever will be with the ballot. The surest safeguard any woman can have is the protection and fidelity of some good man.[180]

In retrospect, it is obvious that these are "famous last words"—the sign of a dying era. Yet, at the time of writing, much of it was true, for without the federal amendment campaign of Alice Paul and the National Woman's Party (NWP), which had a huge influence all over the country and was ultimately successful, it is unlikely that women in Arkansas and the United States generally would have won the vote when they did.

The 1911 attempt to give Arkansas women the vote failed. So did an attempt in 1913. By 1915, the idea had picked up some steam: Arkansas's women had been active for four years and suffrage had become a national issue because of Alice Paul's campaign—at that time through the Congressional Union, later the NWP.

Suffragists packed the galleries in 1915 when the bill was introduced in the Senate. William C. Adamson, a member from Pulaski County, shouted out "No!" to an attempt to postpone discussion, and the women began what was called "a demonstration," applauding and continuing to do so until the chair called for order. The proposal passed, after a debate in which Senator Garrett said, "Here we have in Arkansas 45,000 women earning a living, but they have no voice in state government."[181]

The women and supporters for suffrage thronged the House for the introduction of the bill there. Again there was an attempt to derail it, one member wondering, "What's going to become of our children if the women are at the ballot box?"[182] That was an objection that opponents regularly trotted out to stymie suffrage. Later, the *Arkansas Democrat* reported that "Mrs. O. P. Ellington, Mrs. T. T. Cotnam, Mrs. John Almond, Mrs. L. B. Leigh, Mrs. Minnie I. Rutherford and Mrs. Clarence Rose appeared before the committee and pled for their cause, Mrs. Cotnam, Mrs. Almond, Mrs. Ellington and Mrs. Rutherford making addresses."[183]

On February 3, 1915, the proposed suffrage amendment was still being debated in the House when the secretary of the Federation of Labor filed a petition to include a third amendment on the November ballot, forestalling an opportunity for the suffrage amendment, as the maximum was now reached. "Votes for Women Blocked by ACT Labor Element," read the subhead of the *Arkansas Democrat* story on February 3, 1915. With suffrage safely derailed, the House soon voted in its favor.

The kind of struggle women in Arkansas faced emerges clearly not just from these political machinations, but also from the manner in which it passed. The *Gazette*'s headline on the news stated: "House Hilariously Votes for Suffrage."[184] The story reported:

By a vote of 51 to 18, the house last night, in special session, passed Senate Joint Resolution No. 5 (Garrett) to submit to the people the right of Arkansas women to vote. Thirty-one members of the house were absent, and only by the switching of two votes from "no" to "aye" at the last moment was the passage of the resolution by a majority of the 100 members made possible…

The galleries were filled with crowds of interested spectators during the night session, but upon the floor considerable hilarity prevailed. During the speeches of some of the members their colleagues continually shouted and laughed at them, and the speaker broke his gavel in fruitless attempt to stop the hilarity…

It was just following a talk against suffrage by Mr. Pierce of Calhoun that Speaker Sawyer announced that Mr. Hatley of Polk, who had filed his way into the legislature, would play for the assembly. Mr. Hatley was asked if he was going to play for or against women suffrage and he answered that he was going to vote for it and that if fiddling would make it win he had plenty of string. He played "The Suffragette March" and "The Arkansaw Traveler."

The *Democrat* reported: "With a pre-arranged program, to a great extent, members of the House had last night's session planned for a vaudeville, and vaudeville it was, for a combination of oratory rich in humor, fiddle playing and wild cheering sent woman suffrage over the line to victory."[185]

The *Democrat* also reported: "There was a joyful demonstration by the throngs of women crowding the House chamber and gallery when L. E. Sawyer, the speaker of the House, announced the suffrage victory…suffragists feel they have gained a great victory. Passage of a suffrage resolution through both branches of the General Assembly is no mean gain in actual support as well as moral influence, they say."[186]

In 1915, therefore, the Equal Franchise amendment to the state constitution passed—but it was an empty victory. In 1917, however, a move to give women the vote for primary elections arose. The idea of primary suffrage's origin is disputed in suffrage history, but the idea had emerged partly because a limited suffrage could be enacted without a state constitutional amendment. Since 1916, in response to the pressure for a federal amendment from Alice Paul and the NWP national campaign, the National American Woman Suffrage Association (NAWSA) had abandoned its support for state-by-state amendments only and encouraged its affiliate organizations to go for whatever kind of suffrage they could get. The bill introducing primary suffrage passed in March 1917, making Arkansas the first southern state where women won the vote.

The *Gazette* of June 5, 1919, marked the start of the women's final campaign for equal suffrage in the state with a front-page story saying that the U.S. Senate had approved women's suffrage and "ends a fight of 40 years." Actually, it was much more than that, for women had first called for the right to vote at the Seneca Falls Convention in 1848. With this news, however, in Arkansas, Fort Smith suffragists immediately began working for a special session of the General Assembly to ratify, and the Equal Suffrage State Central Committee soon took up the call. When the amendment came up for a vote, Senator Emory tried to kill it by proposing that ratification should be submitted for a vote by women alone for approval. This idea failed. The most thrilling moment occurred on July 28, 1919, when the General Assembly finally ratified the 19th Amendment to the U.S. Constitution, guaranteeing women the right to vote. Arkansas was the second state in the South to ratify, marking one-third of the way to national ratification.

"SUFFRAGE IS RATIFIED BY LEGISLATURE—Both Houses Vote Overwhelmingly for Amendment—ARKANSAS IS 12TH—Vote is 29 to 2 in the Senate and 75 to 17 in the House" was the front-page headline in the *Arkansas Gazette* on July 29, 1919. For the vote, the article read, "women came to Little Rock from many points in the state and filled the corridors of the statehouse before the hour set for convening the legislature. Each carried a yellow banner, bearing the familiar slogan, 'Votes for women,' and made bright, inspiring pictures as they grouped before the doors of the Senate and House chambers. At least 100 of them stopped at the governor's office to thank him for calling the special and to predict a victory...more opposition developed than the suffragists anticipated, but ratification was never in jeopardy.[187]

On July 28, 1919, Arkansas became the second state in the South to ratify the 19th Amendment to the U.S. Constitution. The State Capitol was packed with women for the historic event, and this official photograph marked the occasion. (Courtesy of the Arkansas History Commission, Little Rock, Arkansas)

Mrs. T. T. Cotnam was an early leader of Little Rock and Arkansas suffragists, and later a national campaigner who helped New York women win the vote in 1917. Arguing for votes for women, she was the first woman in Arkansas to address the legislators in the State Capitol. (Source: *Gazette* Centennial Commemorative Issue 1919, Author's Collection)

Chapter 24:
Memorials to the Suffragists

There is no physical memorial to the Arkansas suffragists who fought for women's right to vote nearly a century ago. This is unfortunate, for the 19th Amendment represented the enfranchisement of half the population and included all races, with the national struggle ending in victory after seventy-two years. In Arkansas, the struggle effectively took fifty-two years, from 1868 to 1920 when the 19th Amendment became part of the U.S. Constitution. Individual graves mark where some of the suffragists are buried, but most of the suffragists to this day remain nameless and faceless, and finding their graves is likely impossible.

Clara McDiarmid, Bernie Babcock, and Kate Cuningham are buried in Oakland Fraternal Cemetery in southeastern Little Rock. Adolphine Fletcher Terry is buried in Mount Holly Cemetery in Little Rock. Mrs. Chester Jennings, called the "keeper of the light" for managing to get occasional articles on suffrage published in various state newspapers between 1899 and 1911, is also buried there,[188] as is Mary Loughborough, who ran the *Southern Ladies' Journal* from 1884 to 1887. Terry's suffragist friend Josephine Miller Brown is buried in Calvary Cemetery. Some of these graves are linked to an audio tour accessible by cell phone, which at least gives some context, as there is a lack of information on most of the markers.

Many, if not most, of the buildings where the women worked in pursuit of suffrage are gone, replaced by newer buildings, or they are now parking lots or concrete parking garages. The suffragists' work, whether they supported only the state-by-state approach or the federal amendment approach, led to the largest enfranchisement ever in U.S.

history. According to the U.S. Census of 1920, about 26,500,000 women won the right to vote from the 19th Amendment in 1920.[189]

But no memorial exists to commemorate collectively the workers who endured ridicule, endless opposition, and sometimes torture in order to gain political liberty and equality by winning the most important civil right that any citizen can have. The longest civil rights campaign in U.S. history was also the first successful non-violent civil rights campaign in America's history. Yet, as the nineteenth-century suffragists knew, the vote was only a first step—there was still the rest of women's inequality to tackle. More than a decade into the twenty-first century, that work is not yet completed. Alice Paul launched the Equal Rights Amendment (ERA) in 1923. As of 2015, it is still not ratified.

As the ERA plods on through the most difficult constitutional amendment process of any nation, the campaign for equality under the law "on account of sex" has already taken much longer than the campaign for the vote did to reach victory. The more things change, it seems, the more they stay the same.

Endnotes

1. The author's analysis of women's struggle for the vote and the struggle's national import, *Alice Paul, the National Woman's Party and the Vote: The First Civil Rights Struggle of the 20th Century*, was published by McFarland Publications in Jefferson, North Carolina, in April 2015.

2. Geoffrey C. Ward and Ken Burns, *Not for Ourselves Alone: Elizabeth Cady Stanton and Susan B. Anthony* (New York: Alfred A. Knopf, 1999). This is the book to accompany Burns's documentary of the same name.

3. See Rosemarie Zagarri's *Revolutionary Backlash: Women and Politics in the Early American Republic* (Philadelphia: University of Pennsylvania Press, 2007); Linda K. Kerber, *No Constitutional Right to be Ladies: Women and the Obligations of Citizenship* (New York: Hill & Wang, 1998); and Linda K. Kerber, *Women of the Republic* (Chapel Hill: University of North Carolina Press, 1980).

4. Celia Morris, *Fanny Wright: Rebel in America* (Urbana and Chicago: University of Illinois Press, 1992).

5. *Plessy v. Ferguson*, 163 U.S. 537 (1896).

6. Susan B. Anthony, "Address of Susan B. Anthony Delivered in Twenty-nine of the Post Office Districts of Monroe, and twenty-one of Ontario, in her canvass of those Counties, prior to her trial in June, 1873," in Susan B. Anthony, *The Trial of Susan B. Anthony* (Amherst, New York: Humanity Books, 2003), 170.

7. *Minor v. Happersett*, 88 U.S. 162 (1875).

8. *Arkansas Gazette*, June 15, 1966, 8A.

9. See the July 2001 survey conducted by Opinion Research Corporation (ORC) CARAVAN Services for the Equal Rights Amendment Campaign Network. Its first finding stated: "Overwhelmingly, Americans agree that male and female citizens should have equal rights, and the vast majority of Americans want those rights guaranteed by the US Constitution. Most, however, mistakenly assume that the Constitution already guarantees those rights." See http://2passera.org/survey.shtml (accessed August 1, 2015).

10. Ida Husted Harper, "Arkansas," in *History of Woman Suffrage, Vol. VI, 1900–1920*, (New York: National American Woman Suffrage Association, 1922), 16–26.

11. Inez Haynes Irwin, *The Story of Alice Paul and the National Woman's Party* (New York: Harcourt, Brace and Company, 1951, and Washington DC: National Woman's Party, 1964 and 1977), 301. Details in older women's histories are sometimes incorrect, as with this reference to the Court House. While the story of what happened is important, local sources were clear that the intended location of Vernon's meeting was City Hall.

12. By the end of 1912, women had equal suffrage in Wyoming (1869, as a state 1890); Colorado (1893); Utah (1896); Idaho (1896); Washington (1910); California (1911); Arizona, Kansas, and Oregon (1912). The actual history of winning suffrage in each state is unique.

13. *The Suffragist*, December 9, 1916, 7; Mary Walton, *A Woman's Crusade: Alice Paul and the Battle for the Ballot* (New York: Palgrave Macmillan, 2010).

14. See Katherine H. Adams and Michael L. Keene, *Alice Paul and the American Suffrage Campaign* (Urbana and Chicago: University of Illinois Press, 2008).

15. *Arkansas Gazette*, April 20, 1917. In this news report, Miller's colleague is named as "Gertrude Robinson." This is very likely an error, as Miller's close NAWSA colleague since 1916 had been Gertrude Watkins. Other women in this new war work field were Miss Reoffa Ranfall (Conway); Mrs. J. W. Bryant (El Dorado); and Mrs. Joe S. Elliot (Fordyce).

16. *Arkansas Gazette*, April 4, 1917, 4.

17. *Arkansas Gazette*, April 3, 1918.

18. *Arkansas Gazette*, April 3, 1918, 10.

19. *Minor v. Happersett*, 88 U.S. 162 (1875).

20. Evin Demirel, "Marker Dedicated to Puerto Rican Immigrants Sparks a Historical Rediscovery," *Sync Weekly*, July 10, 2012, http://www.syncweekly.com/news/2012/jul/10/arkansas-mystery/ (accessed May 25, 2015).

21. *The Suffragist*, December 9, 1916, 7; Walton, *A Woman's Crusade*.

22. As they are still living in a protectorate today, Puerto Ricans' voting rights are not the same as the voting rights of American citizens living in the fifty states.

23. From an unnamed 1918–19 document from the U.S. Ordnance Department, quoted in Demirel, "Arkansas Mystery."

24. A. Hall Allen, "It's Nice to Remember," *Quapaw Quarter Chronicle* (November/December 1977): 5.

25. Southern Directory Company, *Little Rock City Directory*, 1920, 288.

26. *Woman's Journal* (Boston) 19 (March 10, 1888): 82, referenced in Elizabeth A. Taylor, "The Woman Suffrage Movement in Arkansas," *Arkansas Historical Quarterly* 15, no. 1 (Spring 1956); note: the names for the suffrage organizations of the 1890s are sometimes difficult to determine and standardize. Generally, the AESA is the Little Rock group whereas the AWSA is the state affiliate of the national group.

27. Mrs. T. T. Cotnam, *History of Women's Suffrage in Arkansas*, 1919. Online at http://www.arkansasties.com/Special/HistoryofWomens Suffrage.htm (accessed May 25, 2015).

28. Taylor, "Arkansas Woman Suffrage Movement," 13.

29. *Arkansas Press City Directory* 1890, 298.

30. *Woman's Journal* (Boston) 20 (February 9, 1889): 44–45; *Woman's Chronicle*, February 16, 1889, 3.

31. See Sanborn Map No. 11, 1897.

32. *Arkansas Gazette*, April 20, 1917, 8.

33. Steven G. and Ray Hanley, *Around Little Rock: A Postcard History* (Mount Pleasant, SC: Arcadia Publishing, 1998), 62.

34. James M. Pomeroy, *Constitution of the State of Arkansas* (Little Rock: 1868 Constitutional Convention of Arkansas, 1870), http://www.archive.org/details/cu31924032658506 (accessed May 26, 2015).

35. Elizabeth Cady Stanton, Susan B. Anthony, and Matilda Jocelyn Gage, eds., *History of Woman Suffrage, Vol. III, 1876–1885* (Rochester, NY: Susan B. Anthony, 1886), 805–6.

36. *Early Suffrage Organizations Exhibit*, Old State House, Little Rock, Arkansas (no longer available).

37. Carrie Chapman Catt and Nettie Rogers Shuler, *Woman Suffrage and Politics: The Inner Story of the Suffrage Movement* (New York: Charles Scribner's Sons, 1923 and Seattle: University of Washington Press Americana Library, 1969), Chapter 9 107–8.

38. See "Early Twentieth Century, 1901–1940," Encyclopedia of Arkansas History & Culture, http://www.encyclopediaofarkansas.net/encyclopedia/entry-detail.aspx?entryID=403 (accessed May 25, 2015).

39. *Chrisman v. Partee*, 38 Ark. 1881, 31 and *Felkner v. Tighe*, 39 Ark. 1882, 357. See "Early Twentieth Century, 1901–1940," Encyclopedia of Arkansas History & Culture.

40. Anthony, *Trial*; *Minor v. Happersett*, 88 U.S. 162 (1875).

41. *Arkansas Gazette*, April 30, 1893, 13.

42 Walton, *A Woman's Crusade*, 96–98; *Arkansas Gazette*, May 1–3, 1914; *Arkansas Democrat*, May 9, 1914.

43. *The Suffragist*, February 5, 1916.

44. *Arkansas Gazette*, February 22, 1889, 4.

45. Ida Husted Harper, *The Life and Work of Susan B. Anthony* (Indianapolis and Kansas City: Bowen-Merrill Company, 1899), 2 vols., vol. I, 137.

46. Kathleen Barry, *Susan B. Anthony: The Biography of a Singular Feminist* (New York: Ballantine Books, 1988).

47. Anthony, *Trial*; *Minor v. Happersett*, 88 U.S. 162 (1875); "Women Who Voted, 1868–73," Rutgers University, the Elizabeth Cady Stanton and Susan B. Anthony Papers Project, http://ecssba.rutgers.edu/resources/voters.html, sorted by date (accessed May 26, 2015).

48. *Woman's Chronicle*, March 2, 1889, 2; *Woman's Chronicle*, February 23, 1889.

49. *Woman's Chronicle*, February 23, 1889.

50. The announcement of the change of venue in the religious column of the *Arkansas Gazette*, February 24, 1889, 5, is confusing. It stated that the lecture would take place "at 4 p.m. at the opera house on West Markham." The Capital Theater was previously known as Hyde's Opera House.

51. See biography at the end of Clara A. McDiarmid, "Our Neighbors, The Alaskan Women," in Mary Kavanaugh Oldham, ed., *The Congress of Women: Held in the Woman's Building, World's Columbian Exposition, Chicago, U. S. A., 1893* (Chicago, IL: Monarch Book Company, 1894), 723–26; Bernadette Cahill, *Clara McDiarmid at Home: Suffrage and Society in Fin de Siècle Little Rock, Arkansas*, unpublished manuscript.

52. Jane A. Wilkerson, "Little Rock Woman's Christian Temperance Union, 1888–1903," MA thesis, University of Arkansas at Little Rock, 2009; Salena G. Copeland, "Clara Cox McDiarmid, Arkansan Suffragist and Lawyer," in *Women's Legal History* (Stanford, CA: Stanford University, Babcock and Wayne, 2006).

53. Wilkerson, "Little Rock WCTU."

54. *Woman's Chronicle*, March 3, 1888, 4; June 2, 1888, 2.

55. *Arkansas Gazette*, March 16, 1911, 3.

56. Letter to Adolphine Fletcher Terry from Senator James P. Clarke, dictated April 28, 1910, University of Arkansas at Little Rock Center for Arkansas History and Culture, UALR.0018, Series I, Box 5, File 6.

57. Terry spoke of this many years later. See Stephanie Bayless, *Obliged to Help: Adolphine Fletcher Terry and the Progressive South* (Little Rock: Butler Center Books, 2011), 84. For the cemetery story, see Linda J. Lumsden, *Inez: The Life and Times of Inez Milholland* (Bloomington: Indiana University Press, 2004), 1–2.

58. Robert P. J. Cooney Jr. and the National Women's History Project, *Winning the Vote: The Triumph of the American Woman Suffrage Movement* (Santa Cruz, CA: American Graphic Press, 2005), 105, 127.

59. "Suffragette Tells of Forcible Feeding," *New York Times*, February 18, 1910. This article focuses on the force-feeding that Alice Paul experienced and does not mention parades.

60. Steven G. and Ray Hanley, "Around Little Rock," 71.

61. See Michael Hibblen, "Hopes of Saving Pine Bluff's Historic, but Crumbling Hotel Pines," University of Arkansas at Little Rock Public Radio, http://ualrpublicradio.org/post/hopes-saving-pine-bluffs-historic-crumbling-hotel-pines (accessed May 26, 2015).

62. Harper, "Arkansas," *Woman Suffrage*, 16–26.

63. *Arkansas Gazette*, January 25, 1916, 14.

64. *Arkansas Gazette*, January 26, 1916, 1.

65. *Arkansas Democrat*, January 26, 1916, 4.

66. *Arkansas Gazette*, April 2, 1916, 21.

67. *Arkansas Gazette*, March 7, 1917, 1.

68. *Arkansas Gazette*, March 6, 1917, 5.

69. *Arkansas Gazette*, November 9, 1917, 1.

70. "Greatest Victory Yet for Suffrage," *Arkansas Gazette*, November 14, 1917, 4.

71. *Arkansas Gazette*, November 19, 1917, 8.

72. *Arkansas Gazette*, July 28, 1919, 7.

73. *Arkansas Gazette*, August 3, 1919, 7.

74. *Arkansas Gazette*, June 15, 1966, 8A.

75. Bernadette Cahill, "Stepping Outside the Bounds of Convention: Adolphine Fletcher Terry and Radical Suffragism in Little Rock, 1911–1920," *Pulaski County Historical Review* 60 (Winter 2012): 122–29. See also Bayless, *Obliged to Help*, 81–83, which is based on Bayless's "A Southern Paradox: The Social Activism of Adolphine Fletcher Terry," MA thesis, University of Arkansas at Little Rock, 2006.

76. *Arkansas Democrat*, April 25, 1900, 4.

77. *Arkansas Democrat*, April 26, 1900, 8.

78. *Arkansas Gazette*, May 2, 1914, 7.

79. *Arkansas Gazette*, May 3, 1914, 1.

80. *Arkansas Gazette*, May 3, 1914, 1. The news report cuts off at "Miss Joseph…" and does not continue elsewhere. Josephine Miller, later Mrs. Fred I. Brown, was one of the luncheon committee members mentioned earlier and is likely the one who accompanied the viola solo.

81. Cuningham's name is spelled differently in the various city directories—sometimes as Cuningham and sometimes as Cunningham. The name on her gravestone is Cuningham, which is the spelling for her name throughout this book.

82. *Woman's Journal* (Boston) 20 (February 9, 1889): 44–45; *Woman's Chronicle*, February 16, 1889, 3.

83. *Woman's Chronicle*, July 7, 1888, 4.

84. *Arkansas Press City Directory*, 1893–1894, 140.

85. *Woman's Chronicle*, March 2, 1889, 2.

86. *Arkansas Gazette*, April 30, 1893, 13.

87. *Arkansas Gazette*, January 5, 1870, 4. See also Josh Hart, "Little Rock City Hall," Encyclopedia of Arkansas History & Culture, http://www.encyclopediaofarkansas.net/encyclopedia/entry-detail.aspx?entryID=8147 (accessed May 26, 2015).

88. Matthew J. Sanders, "An Introduction to Phoebe Wilson Couzins," *Women's Legal History Biography Project* (Stanford, CA: Stanford University, 2000), 3–8, online at http://wlh-static.law.stanford.edu/papers/CouzinsP-Sanders00.pdf (accessed May 26, 2015).

89. Susan B. Anthony and Ida Husted Harper, *History of Woman Suffrage*, Vol. IV, 1883–1900 (Rochester, NY: Susan B. Anthony, 1902), 475.

90. Sanders, "Phoebe Wilson Couzins," 5, n. 13.

91. *Arkansas Gazette*, July 14, 1888, 5.

92. Wilkerson, "Little Rock WCTU," 25.

93. *Arkansas Ladies' Journal*, November 1, 1884, 8; January 31, 1885, 8; *The Life of Little Rock*, May 22, 1887, 3; *Woman's Chronicle*, March 3, 1888, 4.

94. Wilkerson, "Little Rock WCTU," 2.

95. See Dorsey D. Jones, "Catherine Campbell Cuningham: Advocate of Equal Rights for Women," *Arkansas Historical Quarterly* 13 (Summer 1953): 85–90; Taylor, "Woman Suffrage Movement in Arkansas," 17–52.

96. Stanton, Anthony, and Gage, *Woman Suffrage*, III, 805–6.

97. *Woman's Chronicle*, March 3, 1888, 4.

98. *Woman's Chronicle*, June 2, 1888, 2.

99. *Woman's Chronicle*, May 19, 1888, 4.

100. Steven G. and Ray Hanley, "Around Little Rock," 61.

101. Harper, "Arkansas," *Woman Suffrage*, VI, 16–26.

102. *Arkansas Gazette*, April 1, 1916, 3.

103. *Polk Little Rock Directory*, 1917; Sanborn Map, 1917.

104. *Arkansas Gazette*, February 26, 1911, 1.

105. Harper, "Arkansas," *Woman Suffrage*, VI, 16–26.

106. *Arkansas Gazette*, March 6, 1917, 5.

107. *Arkansas Gazette*, March 6, 1917, 5.

108. *Arkansas Gazette*, November 19, 1917, 8.

109. *Arkansas Gazette*, November 21, 1917, 14.

110. Irwin, "*Alice Paul*," 30. This reference to the Court House is incorrect. Local sources were clear that the intended location of Vernon's meeting was City Hall.

111. See "Royal Arcanum," *Freemasonry and Fraternal Organizations* at http://www.stichtingargus.nl/vrijmetselarij/arcanum_en.html; and "Royal Arcanum: A Proud History," http://www.royalarcanum.com/ourhistory.html (both accessed May 26, 2015).

112. *The Guardian*, April 29, 1916, 2, in Arkansas Catholic Archive at http://arc.stparchive.com/Archive/ARC/ARC04291916p02.php (accessed May 26, 2015).

113. *Polk's Little Rock City Directory* 1917, 50.

114. *Sholes' Directory of the City of Little Rock 1883-4*, A. E. Sholes, publisher, 271.

115. Janie Synatzske Evins, "Arkansas Women: Their Contribution to Society, Politics, and Business, 1865–1900," *Arkansas Historical Quarterly* 44, no. 2 (Summer 1985): 118–133.

116. *Woman's Journal* (Boston) 16 (November 21, 1885): 370, quoted in Taylor, "Arkansas Woman Suffrage Movement," 3.

117. *Arkansas Gazette*, April 18, 1886, 1.

118. *Arkansas Gazette*, April 18, 1886, 1.

119. *Woman's Journal* (Boston) 17 (December 18, 1886): 405, cited in Taylor, "Arkansas Woman Suffrage Movement," 3.

120. See *Little Rock Ladies' Journal* 1, no. 9 (June 21, 1884): 68.

121. 1886 Sanborn Map; also the *Little Rock City Directory* of 1885 lists the Wilson & Webb address as 210 Main Street.

122. Mention of the "up-town office" is in a story about the opening of the Women's Exchange in the *Arkansas Ladies' Journal* of September 26, 1885. In the *Journal* of November 21, 1885, 5, it is further specified as the "printing office, corner Ninth and Main Streets."

123. *Southern Ladies' Journal*, December 11, 1886, 2.

124. *Little Rock City Directory 1887* (Little Rock: Arkansas Gazette), 155.

125. *Little Rock City Directory 1887*, 320

126. *Arkansas Gazette*, August 28, 1887, 4.

127. Issues of the *Journal* are on microfilm at the Arkansas History Commission in Little Rock.

128. *Woman's Chronicle*, March 3, 1888, 1; Taylor, "Arkansas Woman Suffrage Movement," 3, n. 10.

129. *Arkansas Gazette*, April 26, 1900, 3.

130. *Arkansas Democrat*, April 25, 1900, 4.

131. *Arkansas Democrat City Directory* 1900, 586; Sanborn 1897 Map 16.

132. *Arkansas Democrat*, April 26, 1900, 8.

133. *Arkansas Democrat*, April 25, 1900, 4.

134. *Arkansas Gazette*, February 9, 1919, 30.

135. *Woman's Journal* (Boston) 19 (March 10, 1888): 82.

136. *Arkansas Ladies' Journal*, October 10, 1885, 3.

137. *Dow's Little Rock City Directory*, 339.

138. Cahill, "Terry and Radical Suffragism in Little Rock."

139. Harper, "Arkansas," *Woman Suffrage*, 16–26.

140. Suffrage Speech, unknown author, no date, Arkansas Small Manuscript Materials File #75, Butler Center for Arkansas Studies, Little Rock, Arkansas. Mrs. T. T. Cotnam's name and a date of February 5, 1915, are written on the speech. These, however, may be wrong, both because of third-person references to Mrs. Cotnam in the text and the fact that the date is on an insert for p. 2 paragraph 2 of the speech. References to 1918 and the Federal Amendment in the speech indicate a date after January 1918.

141. Harper, "Arkansas," *Woman Suffrage*, 16–26.

142. *Arkansas Gazette*, April 2, 1916, 21.

143. *Arkansas Gazette*, January 26, 1916, 1.

144. *Arkansas Gazette*, November 10, 1917, 1.

145. *Arkansas Gazette*, November 14, 1917, 11.

146. Bayless, *Obliged to Help*, 79–80; Bernadette Cahill, "Terry and Radical Suffragism in Little Rock."

147. Mrs. S. S. Wassell, "History of Equal Suffrage Movement in Arkansas: An Account of the Patient, Persistent Efforts for the Emancipation of Women, From Pioneer Days to the Present," *Arkansas*

Gazette, February 9, 1919, 30. Note that the date of the page of the article is February 7, 1919, but it is part of the February 9, 1919, edition of the newspaper.

148. Anthony and Harper, *History of Woman Suffrage*, IV, 475. This author, in her book *Alice Paul, the National Woman's Party and the Vote: The First Civil Rights Struggle of the 20th Century* (Jefferson, NC: McFarland, 2015), places this reported suffrage march in its national context.

149. *Arkansas Gazette*, May 2, 1914, 7.

150. *Arkansas Gazette*, April 1, 1916, 3.

151. *Arkansas Democrat*, October 17, 1916, 1, 5.

152. *Arkansas Gazette*, March 7, 1917, 1.

153. *Arkansas Gazette*, November 10, 1917, 1.

154. *Arkansas Gazette*, November 11, 1917, 27.

155. *Arkansas Gazette*, November 11, 1917, 27.

156. *Arkansas Gazette*, November 21, 1917, 14.

157. *Arkansas Gazette*, November 21, 1917, 14.

158. *Arkansas Gazette*, July 24, 1919, 8.

159. *Little Rock City Directory*, 1916.

160. *Arkansas Gazette*, July 20, 1919, 13.

161. *Arkansas Gazette*, July 27, 1919, Part II, 18.

162. *Woman's Journal* (Boston) 19 (March 10, 1888): 82.

163. Depository Records of the Freedman's Bank (Little Rock), Record No. 264, May 8, 1871, Arkansas History Commission, Little Rock, Arkansas.

164. Kansas State Board of Agriculture Census 1865, Ottumwa Township, Coffey County, Kansas, enumerated May 31, 1865.

165. *Woman's Chronicle*, February 14, 1891, 4.

166. *Woman's Chronicle*, August 3, 1889, 2.

167. See, for example, the *Arkansas Ladies' Journal*, April 18, 1885, 8; *Woman's Chronicle*, April 2, 1892, 1.

168. *Woman's Chronicle*, October 31, 1891, 4.

169. Sources use a variety of names for the suffrage groups in Arkansas at this time. Women created not only local groups, like Little Rock's AESA, but also a state group that affiliated with the national suffrage organization, although the exact history of this aspect of the history is as yet unclear. To avoid confusion, this text has used AESA for the local group and Arkansas Woman Suffrage Association for the state group.

170. *Little Rock City Directory*, 1890, 143.

171. *Woman's Chronicle*, February 16, 1889, 3.

172. *Arkansas Gazette*, January 21, 1911, 3.

173. *Arkansas Democrat*, January 21, 1911, 2.

174. American men, both black and white, plus immigrant males who became citizens—or, in some cases, simply declared their intention of becoming a citizen—could vote after the passage of the Reconstruction Amendments. Certain groups then and over time, however, were excluded because of race: Native Americans, for example, and the Chinese and Japanese. Black men and many poor whites were increasingly kept from voting by such "petty freaks and cunning devices"—to quote Susan B. Anthony—as literacy tests and the poll tax. Women, as suffragists often pointed out, were classed with traitors, felons, idiots, vagrants, and the insane in voting rights.

175. *Arkansas Gazette*, February 19, 1911, 1.

176. *Arkansas Gazette*, February 19, 1911, 1.

177. *Arkansas Gazette*, February 19, 1911, 1.

178. *Arkansas Gazette*, February 19, 1911, 1.

179. *Arkansas Democrat*, February 15, 1911, 4.

180. *Arkansas Democrat*, February 15, 1911, 4.

181. *Arkansas Democrat*, February 1, 1915, 4; *Arkansas Gazette*, February 2, 1915, 3.

182. *Arkansas Democrat*, February 3, 1915, 1 and 8.

183. *Arkansas Democrat*, February 3, 1915, 1 and 8.

184. *Arkansas Gazette*, February 6, 1915, 1.

185. *Arkansas Democrat*, February 6, 1915, 1.

186. *Arkansas Democrat*, February 6, 1915, 1.

187. *Arkansas Gazette*, August 3, 1919, Part II, 10.

188. Harper, "Arkansas," *Woman Suffrage*, VI, 16–26.

189. "26,500,000 Women in U.S. Eligible to Vote: Census Bureau Estimates 31,500,000 Men Will Go to Polls," *Arkansas Democrat*, October 8, 1920, 8.

Appendix I

Arkansas Suffragists to ca. 1900 compiled from newspapers of the time

Babcock, Mrs. Bernie

Beattie, Mrs. (no name)

Brooks, Dr. (or Mrs.) Ida Joe

Brooks, Mrs. Mary Burt

Brown, Miss Lura E.

Cady, Mrs. M. M.

Cahoon, Mrs. Harriet Holt

Cantrell, Miss Bessie

Cantrell, Mrs. W. A. (Ellen Maria Harrell?)

Chunn, Mrs. Fannie L. (sometimes Miss)

Cooper, Dr. (no name)

Couzins, Miss Phoebe

Coy, Mrs. (no name)

Cuningham, Miss Kate (President, Little Rock Suffrage
    Association, 1891)

Dodge, Mrs. R. L.

Edmison, Mrs. H. P.

Fyler, Mrs. Lizzie D. (see Tyler)

Gibb, Mrs. E. W.

Harris, Mrs. (no name)

Hart, Mrs. (also State WCTU)

Hart, Sarah K.

Holt, Mrs. W. S.

Jenkins, Addie, (Mrs. A. B.?) (President, Little Rock Suffrage
　　Association, 1891)

Jennings, Mrs. Chester

Johnson, Katie Cox

Johnson, Mrs.

Johnston, Kate L.

Knapp, Mrs. Gilbert T.

Loughborough, Miss Jean

Loughborough, Miss Jentie

Loughborough, Mrs. Mary

McDiarmid, Clara (President, Arkansas Equal Suffrage Association)

McRae, Mrs. Margaret, White County ca. 1848

Miller, Mrs. A.

Offley, Miss Ann

Palmer, Mrs. J. L.

Phillips, Miss Kate

Powers, Mrs. (no name)

Tate, Mrs. Sam

Thompson, Mrs. A. J. (Emma?)

Thompson, Mrs. Emma

Thomson, Mrs. Alice

Turner, Mrs. Carrie

Tyler, Mrs. Lizzie D. (see Fyler)

Vaughan, Mrs. Myra (MacAlmont)

Wallace, Mrs.

Wallace, Sena H.

Warner, Mrs. Myra

Woodruff, Miss Georginne

Mrs. Wassell's February 7–9, 1919, article in the *Arkansas Gazette* also
mentions a "Mrs. Martin and her sister, Mrs. Cox."

Appendix II

Suffragists in Arkansas, 1911–1919, compiled from newspaper references of the time

Abeles, Mrs. Theo

Alexander, J. R. (Jefferson County)

Almond (also Almand), Mrs. John P. (Pine Bluff)

Aubrey, Miss Ledas

Aubrey, Mrs. L. E. (Faulkner County)

Barnes, Mrs. Fannie Martin (Cross County)

Baucum, Miss Margaret

Beard, Mrs. D. A.

Blaisdell, Mrs. L. G. (Hot Springs)

Boyce, Miss Grace

Bracey, Miss Catherine

Buzbee, Miss Martha

Cate, Mrs. E. E. (Craighead County)

Chambers, Miss H.

Cline, Miss Sarah

Coleman, Miss Ann

Coleman, Miss Polly

Coleman, Mrs. Charles F.

Cornish, Miss Mildred

Cotnam, Miss Nell

Cotnam, Mrs. T. T. (Thomas Taylor; Florence) (President,
     Little Rock Political Equality League)

Cunningham, Mrs. George E. (or B.)

Curren, Miss Hattie

Drennan, Mrs. Leonard (Mary Fletcher?)

Drennan, Mrs. O. T. (Hot Springs)

Dungan, Miss Dorothy

Edmonson, Miss Frances

Ellington, Mrs. T. J.

Ellington, Mrs. O. F. (Alice Sankey) (President, Arkansas Woman
    Suffrage Association)

Ells, Mrs. William (Miller County)

Emerson, Miss Gladys

English, Miss Marguerite (See Hussman?)

Erickson, Mrs. Jennie

Fitzhugh, Mrs. Rufus

Fletcher, Miss Mary (See also Drennan) (President, Women's Political
    Equality League)

Floyd, Pauline (El Dorado)

Fodrea, Miss Genevieve

Fones, Mrs. Effie Cline

Gatlin, Miss Alice

Gibb, Mrs. E. W. (F. W?) (Frank W.)

Gibson, Louise (Louisa)

Greer, Mrs. Bea F. (Carroll County)

Harper, Mrs. Clio

Hart, Mrs. J.C.

Hayes, Miss Catherine

Hayes, Mrs.

Head, Mrs. James D. (Texarkana)

Head, Mrs. Samuel

Henderson, Mrs. DeMatt

Hopkins, Mrs. (no first name)

Hoskins, Mrs. Helen

Houston, Miss Julia Houston (Pine Bluff)

Howell, Miss Clara

Hussman, Marguerite (See M. English?)

Hutton, Miss Norma

Hutton, Mrs. Norma (Miss?)

Hutton, Mrs. W. P.

Janson, Mrs. C. F.

Jarrell, Miss Ruby

Jarrett, Mrs. (Edward M.) (Faith?) (State Chair, Congressional Union 1916/NWP)

Jarrett, Mrs. Edgar M.

Johnson, Miss Adele (Hot Springs)

Johnson, Mrs. Adele (Hot Springs)

Jordan, Miss Effie

Keith, Miss Johnnie

Knox, Miss Emil(y?)

Land, Mrs. N. F. (Jonesboro)

Leigh, Mrs. J. B. (also L. B.)

Loughborough, Mrs. J. F.

Mann, Miss Elizabeth

Markwell, Mrs. J. W. (Lulu)

Marshall, Mrs. Mary Ellen C.

Maxley, Miss Martha

McDermott, Miss Lucille

Miller, Miss Josephine (Mrs. Fred I. Brown)

Moore, Mrs. E. S.

Moose, Mrs. W. L. (Morrilton)

Morrow, Mrs. N. E. (Fayetteville)

Payne, Mrs. H. R. (Marion County)

Peshakova, Miss Lili

Prothro, Mrs. (Pinnacle)

Ramsey, Miss Jennie

Ramsey, Miss Jessie

Ranch, Miss Julia

Randolph, Mrs. W. B.

Reinman, Miss (no name)

Roberts, Mrs. W. T.

Robinson, Miss Gertrude

Rogoski, Miss Bess

Roll, Mrs. J. T.

Rose, Mrs. Clarence

Rosecrans, Mrs. Ada (Jonesboro)
Ross (or Rose), Mrs. C. E.
Ross, Mrs. Clarence
Russell, Mrs. D. H. (Pine Bluff)
Rutherford, Mrs. Minnie U.
Rutherford-Fuller, Mrs. Minnie (Magazine)
Schoenfeld, Mrs. S.
Schoffner (or Shoffner), Miss Margaret
Scott, Mrs. Drennan
Scott, Mrs. S. P.
Scruggs, Miss Lula
See, Miss Catherine
See, Mrs. Tessie Bell
Sloat, Mrs. C. B.
Stephenson, Mrs. M. T.
Stephenson, Mrs. M. L.
Street, Mrs. Garland (Lake Village)
Sutton, Miss Mildred
Sutton, Mrs. (no name)
Tabor, Mrs. Mamie Lou
Terry, Mrs. David (Adolphine Fletcher)
Tharp, Mrs. W. J.
Thart, Miss Catherine (Tharp?)
Thompson, Miss May
Vaughan, Miss Martha
Vick, Mrs. T. J.
Walker, Miss (no name)
Ward, Miss Louise
Warner, (or Warren?), Miss Julia
Warren, Miss Julia
Warren, Mrs. Chauncey
Wassell, Mrs. S. S.
Watkins, Miss Gertrude
Whipple, Mrs. W. G. (Mary S.?)
Wittenberg, Miss Mabel

Acknowledgements and Call to Action

This book is the first to record so thoroughly the work of Little Rock and Arkansas suffragists and link them to specific places in the state's capital city. In doing this, it reconstructs one of many local stages of the long-running national campaign that led to the largest ever enfranchisement in U.S. history—26,500,000 women. Revealing an important and nearly forgotten layer of life in the city a century ago makes Little Rock feel like a much richer historical place. This history, however, is only a beginning, and I probably have made some errors in my recounting of the history so far, for which I apologize.

This book has been compiled mostly from Little Rock sources but with input from material from farther afield.

Arkansas history has its own women to thank for the best of the local sources: two short-lived gems of their history—the *Arkansas Ladies' Journal* and the *Woman's Chronicle*, in which women recorded their own concerns. They provide an invaluable insight into the lives and aspirations of women of the 1880s and 1890s. Thankfully, the almost complete archives of these journals are on microfilm at the Arkansas History Commission. The other key local sources have been Arkansas's two newspapers—the *Gazette* and the *Democrat*. Arkansas is lucky to have such a record of its history, even if researchers of women's history would wish there had been much more coverage of the aspirations of the women of the state as the story unfolded. The Central Arkansas Library System's excellent collection of microfilm, however, has made research in them a relatively easy, if time-consuming, matter. The Butler Center for Arkansas Studies at the Central Arkansas Library System coupled with the University of Arkansas at Little Rock Center for Arkansas History and Culture are to be congratulated for their excellent collection of documents—personal, organizational, and court, and of city directories; all of these have contributed to the research and compilation of this history. In particular Kaye Lundgren of the UALR Center for Arkansas History and Culture and Alysanne Crymes of the Central Arkansas Library System bent over backward many times helping me find documents and answering queries. I thank them for their invaluable help.

Central to this book are the historic images that accompany the text. Thanks here are due to the Butler Center for the photographs it has made available; to Lauren Jarvis of the Arkansas History Commission for her help in locating photographs and having them scanned; and to Ray Hanley for so readily making available some of his collection of postcard images for the book. The "Images of America" book *Around Little Rock*, which Ray Hanley co-authored with Steven G. Hanley, illustrated by many of those postcards, was a crucial initial guide during this research to finding buildings and places where local women campaigned to win the right to vote.

National women's newspapers and other sources have provided further information, either through interlibrary loan or through help from librarians in several other states in pinning down documentation and images of key events. I am very grateful for this help. In particular, Mary Mark Ockerbloom, the University of Pennsylvania editor of *A Celebration of Women Writers*, provided excellent scans of several images of Arkansas women, while Jennifer Krafchik of the Sewall-Belmont House and Museum in Washington DC also went out of her way to provide the best reproduction possible of a forgotten photograph of Arkansas women's history. I am also grateful for the help of descendants and relatives of Little Rock suffragists who have supplied rare photos that bring some of the women of a century ago to life.

Finally, let me add that this research—never mind this book— would never have seen the light of day if it hadn't been for my husband, Ron Davis, who walked countless miles through the streets of Little Rock helping me find where buildings had been located, taking photographs if they still existed, and having his ear talked off as I recounted who did what where and when for women to win the vote. Thanks are due also to my sister, Dr. Catherine Smith, and her husband, Cairns Mason of Stirling, in Scotland, for always cheering me on and otherwise helping me through countless difficulties.

All history depends on the amount and quality of the documentation available, and this is certainly true of the history of women. Women's history, however, has its own special challenges, including the struggle for its very existence. Butler Center Books and Butler Center staff members Rod Lorenzen and Bob Razer are to be congratulated and commended, therefore, for encouraging and taking up this project. Now that the information is readily available, I hope that Little Rock residents will take note of this largely forgotten history and that it will provide the guidelines for the creation of a historic "Suffrage Walk" through the city and, perhaps, a Women's History Museum in one of the downtown heritage buildings. The panoramic photograph of the suffragists outside the State Capitol after ratification in July 1919 could make a wonderful mural to attract not just viewers, but descendants or other researchers of history to identify the individual women and girls standing on the steps that day.

It is an opportune time for such projects, for three major suffrage centenaries are fast approaching. The first of these is the win by the state's women of primary suffrage in 1917, which made Arkansas the first state in the South to enfranchise women. This measure perhaps compensated for the short-sightedness of the 1868 Constitutional Convention delegates who laughed out of the assembly the idea of votes for women and kept Arkansas from having the accolade of being the first state where the women of the United States became citizens with the right to vote.

The second centenary is Arkansas's ratification in July 1919 of what became the 19th Amendment to the U.S. Constitution, removing the sex disability in voting laws throughout the nation. Arkansas was the twelfth state to ratify the long-fought-for amendment, the second in the South after Texas. Its ratification marked one-third of the way to full ratification of the amendment.

Ratification in 1919, however, did not mean that Arkansas women even then had won equal voting rights: they were still excluded under state laws. Authorities consequently, recognizing what they by then believed was the inevitable, in 1920 included a referendum on women's right to vote under the state's constitution in the November ballot. The results of that referendum had a rocky history, and Arkansas women did not win the vote through the state measure but through the complete ratification of the Nineteenth Amendment in August 1920—the third important approaching centenary for Arkansas women.

Three centenaries marking the drawn-out conclusion of what ultimately was a seventy-two-year-long struggle for the most important right of citizenship in the nation for half of the citizenry deserve some permanent recognition, especially as that struggle marks several other important achievements, primary among them being the fact that the votes-for-women campaign was also the first successful non-violent civil rights struggle in United States history. Its success also was the real start of women's involvement in politics at all levels in the nation. Ultimately it marks the beginning of the progression—still incomplete—toward full equality under the law on account of sex.

Whether any other recognitions are made, however, this book is a permanent record of that suffrage history. The appendices in particular are worthwhile records of Arkansas history: they are lists of mysteries, for they include in most cases just names—and sometimes not even first names or full names—of women who involved themselves even in a small way in the suffrage struggle. They point to further areas of research, particularly in genealogy, perhaps alerting some readers to ancestral involvement in one of the most striking political victories in the nation's history. Equally, it is to be hoped that these two appendices and the preceding descriptions of events will jog memories and produce further information and documentation of many of these women so that future editions of this book may be more comprehensive and even richer in their coverage. If any reader does hold documentation relevant to such continuing research, the Butler Center for Arkansas Studies, housed in the Arkansas Studies Institute building in Little Rock, would be the place to approach to assess its value.

Bibliography

Adams, K. H., and M. L. Keene. *Alice Paul and the American Suffrage Campaign*. Urbana and Chicago: University of Illinois Press, 2008.

Allen, A. H. "It's Nice to Remember." *Quapaw Quarter Chronicle* (December 5, 1977).

Anthony, S. B. *The Trial of Susan B. Anthony* (Classics in Women's Studies ed.). Amherst, NY: Humanity Books, 2003.

Anthony, S. B., and I. H. Harper. *History of Woman Suffrage* (vol. IV). Rochester, New York: Susan B. Anthony, 1902.

Arkansas Catholic Archive (April 29, 1916).

Arkansas Democrat.

Arkansas Democrat City Directory.

Arkansas Gazette.

Arkansas Ladies' Journal.

Arkansas Press City Directory.

Barry, K. *Susan B. Anthony: A Biography of a Singular Feminist*. New York: Ballantine, 1988.

Bayless, S. "A Southern Paradox: The Social Activism of Adolphine Fletcher Terry." MA thesis, University of Arkansas at Little Rock, 2006.

———. *Obliged to Help: Adolphine Fletcher Terry and the Progressive South*. Little Rock: Butler Center Books, 2011.

Cahill, B. *Alice Paul, the National Woman's Party and the Vote: The First Civil Rights Struggle of the 20th Century*. Jefferson, NC: McFarland, 2015.

———. "Clara Alma Cox McDiarmid, 1847–1899," Encyclopedia of Arkansas History & Culture, http://www.encyclopediaofarkansas.net/encyclopedia/entry-detail.aspx?entryID=8425 (accessed June 3, 2015).

———. "Clara McDiarmid at Home: Suffrage and Society in Fin de Siècle Little Rock." Unpublished manuscript.

———. "Stepping Outside the Bounds of Convention: Adolphine Fletcher Terry and Radical Suffragism in Little Rock, 1911–1920." *Pulaski County Historical Review* 60 (Winter 2012): 122–29.

———. "'Young People Think Women Always Had the Right to Vote': Josephine Miller and the Arkansas Woman Suffrage Campaign." *Pulaski County Historical Review* 61 (2013): 11–15.

Catt, C. C., and N. R. Shuler. *Woman Suffrage and Politics: The Inner Story of the Suffrage Movement.* University of Washington Press Americana Library, 1969 ed. New York: Charles Scribner's Sons, 1923.

Centuries of Citizenship: A Constitutional Timeline. http://constitutioncenter.org/timeline/html/cw08_12159.html (accessed May 25, 2015).

Chrisman v. Partee, 38 Ark. 1881.

Clarke, J. P., Letter to Adolphine Fletcher, 1910. University of Arkansas at Little Rock Center for Arkansas History and Culture.

Cooney, R. P. *Winning the Vote: The Triumph of the American Woman Suffrage Movement.* Santa Cruz, CA: American Graphic Press, 2005.

Cotnam, T. T. *History of Women's Suffrage in Arkansas,* 1919. Online at http://www.arkansasties.com/Special/HistoryofWomensSuffrage.htm (accessed May 25, 2015).

Demirel, E. "Marker Dedicated to Puerto Rican Immigrants Sparks a Historical Rediscovery. *Sync Weekly,* July 10, 2012. Online at http://www.syncweekly.com/news/2012/jul/10/arkansas-mystery/ (accessed May 25, 2015).

Depository Records of the Freedman's Bank, 1871. Little Rock, Arkansas.

Dow's Little Rock City Directory.

"Early Twentieth Century, 1901–1940," Encyclopedia of Arkansas History & Culture, http://www.encyclopediaofarkansas.net/encyclopedia/entry-detail.aspx?entryID=403 (accessed May 25, 2015).

Evins, J. S. "Arkansas Women: Their Contribution to Society, Politics, and Business, 1865–1900." *Arkansas Historical Quarterly* 44, no. 2 (1985): 118–33.

Felkner v. Tighe, 39 Ark. 1882.

Garner, K. V., Director. *Iron Jawed Angels* [Motion Picture], 2004.

The Guardian, Little Rock, Arkansas.

Hamilton, E. M. *Little Rock Photograph Album of the 1890s*. Little Rock: James W. Bell, 1981.

Hanley, R., and S. Hanley. *Main Street Arkansas—The Hearts of Arkansas Cities and Towns as Portrayed in Postcards and Photographs*. Little Rock: Butler Center Books, 2009.

Hanley, S. G., and R. Hanley. *Around Little Rock: A Postcard History*. Mount Pleasant, SC: Arcadia Publishing, 1998.

Harper, I. H. *History of Woman Suffrage, 1900–1920*, Vol. VI. National American Woman Suffrage Association, 1922.

———. *The Life and Work of Susan B. Anthony, Including Public Addresses, Her Own Letters and Many From Her Contemporaries During Fifty Years*. Indianapolis and Kansas City: Bowen-Merrill Company, 1899.

Hart, J. "Little Rock City Hall." Encyclopedia of Arkansas History & Culture, http://www.encyclopediaofarkansas.net/encyclopedia/entry-detail.aspx?entryID=8147 (accessed May 25, 2015).

Hibblen, M. "Hopes of Saving Pine Bluff's Historic, But Crumbling Hotel Pines." University of Arkansas at Little Rock Public Radio, June 15, 2014. Online at http://ualrpublicradio.org/post/hopes-saving-pine-bluffs-historic-crumbling-hotel-pines (accessed May 25, 2015).

Irwin, I. H. *The Story of Alice Paul and the National Woman's Party*. Washington DC: The National Woman's Party, 1964, 1977.

Jones, D. D. "Catherine Campbell Cuningham: Advocate of Equal Rights for Women." *Arkansas Historical Quarterly* 13, no. 2 (1953): 85–90.

Kansas State Board of Agriculture Census. Ottumwa Township, Coffey County, Kansas, 1865.

Kerber, L. K. *No Constitutional Right to Be Ladies: Women and the Obligations of Citizenship*. New York: Hill and Wang, 1998.

Kerber, L. K. *Women of the Republic: Intellect and Ideology in Revolutionary America*. Chapel Hill: University of North Carolina Press, 1980.

Lester, J., and J. Lester. *Greater Little Rock*. Norfolk, VA: Donning Company, 1986.

Little Rock City Directory, 1887.

Little Rock Ladies' Journal.

Lumsden, L. J. *Inez: The Life and Times of Inez Milholland*. Bloomington: Indiana University Press, 2004.

McDiarmid, C. A. "Our Neighbors, The Alaskan Women." In *The Congress of Women: Held in the Woman's Building, World's Columbian Exposition, Chicago, U. S. A., 1893*, by M. K. Oldham, 723–26. Chicago: Monarch Book Company, 1894.

Minor v. Happersett (U.S. Supreme Court 1875).

Morris, C. *Fanny Wright: Rebel in America*. Urbana and Chicago: University of Illinois Press, 1992.

New York Times.

Plessy v. Ferguson, 163 U.S. 537 (1896).

Polk Little Rock Directory.

Pomeroy, J. M. *Constitution of the State of Arkansas (1868)*. Cornell University Library, http://www.archive.org/details/cu31924032658506 (accessed May 25, 2015).

Richards, I. D. *Story of a Rivertown*. Little Rock: Don Richards, 1969.

Roy, F. H., and J. C. Witsell. *How We Lived: Little Rock as an American City*. Little Rock: August House, 1985.

"Royal Arcanum." Freemasonry and Fraternal Organizations, http://www.stichtingargus.nl/vrijmetselarij/arcanum_en.html (accessed May 25, 2015).

Royal Arcanum: A Proud History. http://www.royalarcanum.com/ourhistory.html (accessed May 25, 2015).

Sanborn Maps, Little Rock.

Sanders, M. J. *An Introduction to Phoebe Wilson Couzins*. Women's Legal History Biography Project, 2000. http://wlh-static.law.stanford.edu/papers/CouzinsP-Sanders00.pdf (accessed May 25, 2015).

Sholes' Directory of the City of Little Rock. (1883–4). A. E. Sholes.

Southern Ladies' Journal.

Stanton, E. C., S. B. Anthony, and M. J. Gage. *History of Woman Suffrage, Vol. II, 1861-76*. New York: Fowler & Wells, 1882.

Suffrage Speech (1918?). Arkansas Small Manuscript Materials File #75, Butler Center for Arkansas Studies, Little Rock, Arkansas.

Taylor, E. A. "The Woman Suffrage Movement in Arkansas." *Arkansas Historical Quarterly* 15, no. 1 (1956): 36.

Walton, M. *A Woman's Crusade: Alice Paul and the Battle for the Ballot*. New York: Palgrave Macmillan, 2010.

Ward, G. C., and K. Burns. *Not for Ourselves Alone: Elizabeth Cady Stanton and Susan B. Anthony*. New York: Alfred A. Knopf, 1999.

Wassell, S. "History of Equal Suffrage Movement in Arkansas: An Account of the Patient, Persistent Efforts for the Emancipation of Women, From Pioneer Days to the Present." *Arkansas Gazette*, February 9, 1919, 30.

Wilkerson, J. A. "Little Rock Woman's Christian Temperance Union 1888–1903." MA thesis, University of Arkansas at Little Rock, 2009.

Woman's Chronicle.

Woman's Journal. Boston, Massachusetts.

Zagarri, R. *Revolutionary Backlash: Women and Politics in the Early American Republic*. Philadelphia: University of Pennsylvania Press, 2007.

Index

Page numbers in **bold** *refer to photograph captions.*

About the Author

Bernadette Cahill is an independent scholar who has authored several books—travel and historical. She was born in Scotland and holds an Honours MA in Mediaeval and Modern History from the University of Glasgow. She is also an award-winning watercolorist.

Cahill has written about women's rights and history throughout her professional life and has had many articles published about women's suffrage and the Equal Rights Amendment. Cahill has made presentations about women's rights at academic conferences both in the United States and in Britain. Her appearances in Arkansas have included presentations at the Butler Center's Legacies & Lunch series at the Central Arkansas Library System and the Arkansas Historical Association annual conference. She also spoke about suffrage at the Clinton School of Public Service during the display of the Nineteenth Amendment in the William J. Clinton Presidential Library in October 2012. Her analysis of the importance of the campaigns for votes for women, *Alice Paul, the National Woman's Party and the Vote: The First Civil Rights Struggle of the 20th Century*, was published in 2015 by McFarland Publications of Jefferson, North Carolina.

CPSIA information can be obtained at www.ICGtesting.com
Printed in the USA
LVOW10s0156300815

452055LV00004B/6/P